$2

Western Australian Wildflowers
in colour

Australia, island isolated by sea and time, continent encompassing tropical rainforests and stony desert, mountain peak and sandy plain, has the most diverse flora in the world, and nowhere is this more remarkable than in Western Australia.

The southwest corner of that State is the oldest part of the continent and perhaps the most ancient land surface in the world. Plant life there, untouched by climatic or geological changes throughout countless aeons of time, separated by sea and sand not only from the flora of the world but also from that of the rest of Australia, has developed in a remarkably individual and specialised way. Many species and some genera are entirely confined to the area, some of them to a very limited section, such as the mountain bells (*Darwinia* spp.) of the Stirling Ranges, where each main peak has its own distinctive species.

The northwest botanical province, consisting of coastal sand plains, rugged, forbidding mountain plateaux, and the semi-arid country of the centre, is also remarkable for the number of endemic species. Four thousand million years of seclusion and natural selection have produced native plants which have found a myriad wondrous ways to cope with drought and heat and harsh environments; their bright flamboyant answers are blazoned across the face of the desert after the seasonal rains.

Then there is the tropical north, its flora largely unexplored though with links across the continent desert-denied the rest of the State. With this wealth and diversity, small wonder that the fame of western wildflowers has spread far beyond their frontiers and that botanically the area is one of the most renowned in the world. In this book, twenty-nine families and eighty-four species have been illustrated; many more have been described. But since this constitutes only a small fraction of the total number of Western Australia's flowering plants, it is inevitable that many species—unique, popular, spectacular—have of necessity been omitted. Within the limitation of format we have endeavoured to present a broad pictorial record—to include little known species as well as popular favourites, to give a selection of the main groups and a glimpse of those unique plants which have few parallels anywhere.

Frontispiece: Plate 2
Rosy sunray—*Helipterum roseum*
Text: page 90

Western Australian Wildflowers in colour

BARBARA MULLINS and DOUGLASS BAGLIN

REED

First published in 1978
A. H. & A. W. REED PTY LTD
53 Myoora Road, Terrey Hills, Sydney
65-67 Taranaki Street, Wellington
11 Southampton Row, London
also at
Auckland and Christchurch

National Library of Australia
Cataloguing in Publication data

Mullins, Barbara G.
   Western Australian wildflowers in colour.
   (Reeds colourbook series).
   Index.
   ISBN 0 589 50057 0.
   1. Wild flowers—Western Australia. I. Baglin,
   Douglass, photographer. II. Title. (Series).
582.13'0994'1

Designed by Beryl Green
Set by ASA Typesetters, Sydney
Printed and bound by Dai Nippon Printing Co (Hong Kong) Ltd

CONTENTS

Family LILIACEAE

The Lilies

The lily family is a large one, widespread throughout the world. It numbers in its ranks garden ornamentals such as tulips and hyacinths, and vegetables such as the onion group and asparagus. Members are herbs or occasionally shrubby climbers, usually with bulbs, rhizomes, corms, or with fibrous roots thickened into tubers. Leaves are linear and grass-like, with parallel veins; mostly they grow in a tuft from the base of the plant. Flowers have a calyx of three sepals and a corolla of three petals; often the sepals are petaloid, and in many cases they are almost indistinguishable from the petals. There are usually six stamens and the style is often three-lobed. The ovary is superior, that is, situated above the base of the petals and sepals. Fruit is a capsule or a berry.

There are no true lilies (*Lilium* species) in Western Australia, but the family is represented there by over thirty other genera and about 100 species, the richest development being in the forests and sand plains of the southwest. Included is the monotypic genus, *Calectasia*, now classified by some botanists into a separate family. The single species, *C. cyanea*, is the blue tinsel lily, a small wiry shrub thirty to forty-five centimetres high with stiff crowded heath-like leaves and papery, star-like flowers, solitary at the end of short branchlets. Petals and petaloid sepals are a lustrous deep blue or purple, and anthers are bright gold. It is found mainly on the sand plains of the southwestern corner of Australia, though it extends into South Australia and western Victoria. Another monotypic genus, which is confined to the southwest of Western Australia, is *Agrostocrinum*, with one species, *A. scabrum*, the false blind-grass, sometimes called the bluegrass lily, a tufted perennial herb ten to forty-five centimetres high with grass-like foliage and rich blue flowers which twist into a characteristic spiral after blooming.

The largest Australian genus of the Liliaceae is *Lomandra*, with about thirty species, of which about twenty occur in Western Australia, the majority of them endemic. They are tufted herbs with rush-like leaves and small creamy or yellow fleshy flowers, sometimes sweetly scented.

Plate 3
HOODED LILY—*Johnsonia lupulina*
This is the largest and most commonly seen of the three *Johnsonia* species, all of which are endemic to the sand plains of the southwest. The small flowers are entirely hidden in the conspicuous papery bracts which overlap to form a rosy-tipped nodding spike three to six centimetres long, carried on slender wiry stems up to forty-five centimetres tall. It flowers in spring and early summer and is found in wetter regions on sandy or gravelly soils in open country around Albany.

Plate 4
DRUMSTICKS—*Dasypogon bromeliifolius*
There are two species of *Dasypogon*, both found only in the southwest of Western Australia. The one pictured is a low, tufted shrub with stiff, grass-like leaves, common on sandy soils of the coastal plains. Small white to creamy flowers are carried in a dense globular head on tall erect stems and as they wither look like drumsticks prominent above the foliage.

Plate 5
FRINGE LILY—*Thysanotus* species
Among the loveliest of the native lilies is *Thysanotus*, a genus of about thirty species with its richest development in Western Australia, where twenty-seven species have been described. The delicately margined violet flowers consist of three broad fringed petals and three narrow shining sepals. They occur in clusters of two or three on a long flower stem, and the leaves are grass-like. Roots are tuberous and fruit is a round capsule.

4

5

3

Family HAEMODORACEAE

The Kangaroo paws

This family of lily-like perennial herbs includes the bizarre and spectacular kangaroo paws, which are unique to Western Australia. These plants, with their conspicuous paw-shaped, furry flowers fall into two genera, *Anigozanthos,* with eight species, and *Macropidia,* with one. All species of *Anigozanthos* are confined to the southwest. The distinctive paw-shaped flower clusters and the flower stems are clothed with numerous woolly hairs, and spring from a tuft of smooth grass-like leaves. Calyx and corolla are fused to form a six-lobed elongated tube which , as the flower opens, splits down one side so that the tube becomes flat and ribbon-like, and the perianth lobes roll back to reveal six stamens in orderly row. Colours are dramatic and unusual, and often the furry stems are as colourful as the flowers themselves. *A. manglesii,* the red and green kangaroo paw, is best known and the State's floral emblem. *A. viridis,* the green kangaroo paw, ranges in colour from lemon yellow to deep emerald. *A. rufus,* the red kangaroo paw, has flowerheads and stems clothed in uniform rusty red, and *A. flavidus* is yellow, tinged with red. *A. humilis,* the catspaw, is a smaller plant of the sand plains with flower clusters of orange and gold. The single species of *Macropidia, M. fuliginosa,* is the black kangaroo paw, which has unusual, black-felted, greenish yellow flower clusters. It is closely related to the previous genus, differing mainly in the number of seeds.

Another Western Australian genus of the family Haemodoraceae is *Blancoa,* with one species, *B. canescens,* commonly called the red bugle. Flowers are bell-shaped and covered with soft hairs. They bloom in winter, and for that reason are sometimes known as 'winter bells'. The woolly cottonheads of the genus *Conostylis* also belong to this family. There are about twenty-five species, all endemic to the southwest of Western Australia. They are perennial herbs, mostly tufted, with flat linear leaves and small flowers carried in dense heads.

Plate 6
BLACK KANGAROO PAW—*Macropidia fuliginosa*
This striking plant occurs on the sand plains between Perth and Geraldton. It grows to a metre or so in height and blooms in summer. Flowers, five to six centimetres long, are yellowish-green, with a dense covering of sooty black hair on the stalks and buds.

Plate 7
WHITE COTTONHEADS—*Conostylis setosa*
Like other members of this family, *Conostylis* species have short woolly hairs covering flowers, flower stems and often leaves. The species pictured grows in the Darling Ranges; flowers are white, with the outer surfaces dusted with pink.

Plate 8
RED AND GREEN KANGAROO PAW—
Anigozanthos manglesii
This is the best known and perhaps the most spectacular of the kangaroo paws. It is common on the sandy coastal plains of the southwest, growing in profusion in bushland around the capital city, Perth. Flowers, a brilliant green except for the red ovary at the base, are about seven centimetres long and are borne in terminal racemes on stems up to a metre long and densely coated with red fur.

6

7

8

Family IRIDACEAE

The Iris family

This family includes well known garden plants such as iris, freesia, gladiolus and crocus. It is widespread and found in most parts of the world, most abundantly in South Africa and tropical America. Members are herbs, with corms, tuberous roots or rhizomes. They differ from members of the closely allied Liliaceae in that the ovary (seedbox) is inferior—that is, situated below the petals and sepals—and stamens are three in number. (In Liliaceae there are six stamens.)

In Western Australia the family is represented by two genera of wildflowers—*Patersonia,* the native flag lily, and *Orthrosanthus,* the morning iris. *Patersonia* is the largest genus, with about twenty Australian species, fourteen of which are found in southern Western Australia. They are perennial herbs with tough, grass-like deciduous leaves and underground rhizomes. Flowers are borne in terminal clusters surrounded by two large sheathing bracts from which the flowers arise, one or two at a time, over a period. There are three sepals and three petals; the petals are small and inconspicuous—it is the delicate spreading sepals that form the colourful 'flags'. Fruit is a narrow, triangular capsule which bursts open when ripe, scattering the seeds. Mostly the flowers are mauve or blue; the yellow-flowered *P. xanthina* is an exception.

Plate 9

YELLOW FLAG LILY or NATIVE IRIS— *Patersonia xanthina*

This native iris is the bright harbinger of spring in southwestern Australia, crowding the cool shady depths of jarrah and karri forests from Perth to the south coast. The only yellow-flowered *Patersonia,* its flamboyant flags are will-o'-the-wisps, which appear in profusion, then disappear, only to return within a day, as bountifully as before. The reason for this tantalising behaviour is that each individual flower blooms only a few short hours, opening in the morning and quickly fading in the heat of the noon sun. But each fragile flower is only one of several, tightly packed within the same sheathing bracts. It is quickly replaced by another opening bud, so that to the casual glance it appears as though the withered flower of yesterday has miraculously renewed itself. Flowers of this species are three to four centimetres across, and carried on stalks up to seventy centimetres tall.

Plate 10

MORNING IRIS—*Orthrosanthus* species

As with *Patersonia,* flowers of this genus are enclosed within a terminal spathe, from which several arise over a period. They open in the cool of the morning, and wither in the heat, hence the common name, 'morning iris'. But though the individual flowers last less than a day, they are constantly renewed from the same sheathing bracts, so that the flowering season extends over weeks. The genus *Orthrosanthus* has five species endemic to Australia, all of which grow in southern Western Australia, with some extending to South Australia and Victoria. They are tufted perennial herbs with persistent grass-like leaves, and bear loose panicles of flowers in short spikes. Unlike *Patersonia,* which has only three petal-like perianth segments, petals and sepals of *Orthrosanthus* are of equal size, so that there are six delicate perianth lobes, mostly pale to deep blue in colour.

9

10

Family PROTEACEAE

The Banksia family

The Proteaceae is a large family, almost wholly confined to the southern hemisphere, with its greatest development in Australia. There are over sixty genera and at least 1,500 species, of which more than half the total number of both genera and species are indigenous to Australia, some of the genera and almost all of the indigenous species being confined to this continent. South Africa, with about 600 species, is another major centre of development, and the family is also well represented in South America and New Caledonia.

Only two species occur in New Zealand and the only representatives in the northern hemisphere are a few species of the predominantly New Guinean genus *Helicia,* which range as far northward as India and Japan.

The family name is derived from Proteus, the mythical sea-god of the Greeks, who could change his form at will, an allusion to the amazing diversity found among members. Flowers, foliage, fruit, size and habit differ greatly, even within the same genus. Floral parts are in fours—the perianth petaloid, with four segments (tepals) usually tubular in bud, valvate, separating variously, becoming free or leaving portion of the tube entire or open on one side. The four stamens are situated opposite the flower segments and attached to them, often completely fused so that only the anthers are free. The style is long and usually prominent above the flower; it may be straight or hooked and in some cases the floral tube splits along one side allowing it to protrude in a characteristic loop while the stigma is still held. Within these bounds, however, lies the family's greatest diversity.

14

Banksia has slender, stalkless flowers usually borne in crowded spiralling rows around the thick woody axis of a terminal spike (an exception is the holly-leafed *B. ilicifolia* which carries flowers in dense heads) but species vary in size and colour from the

Plate 14
SCARLET BANKSIA—*Banksia coccinea*
Also known as the waratah banksia and the Albany banksia, *B. coccinea* is common on the exposed coastal sand plains around King George Sound and adjacent districts, and also occurs in the Porongurup and Stirling Ranges, blooming prolifically in moist gullies under the shelter of tall trees. On the coast it flowers from winter to mid-summer, and in the mountains from late spring to autumn. An erect, slender-branched shrub usually about three metres or less high but occasionally growing to five or more metres under ideal conditions, it has squat, almost globular flowerheads about five centimetres in diameter. Flowers are carried in pairs in regular (not spiralling) rows, with each pair overlapping the last rather like roofing tiles on a house. Perianths are softly furred, dove-grey and the long styles are vivid scarlet, tipped with a golden stigma. Each pair of flowers in the regimented rows opens in such a way as to allow the curved styles to protrude in parallel pairs. The tips of the styles remain captive, prisoners of the perianth lobes for a considerable time, so that the squat spikes are dramatically striped by double rows of silvery-grey flowers alternating with double rows of arched, scarlet spines. When the styles are finally released they obscure the flowers and the spike becomes a spectacular brush of gold-tipped scarlet. After the fall of the withered flowers, the fruiting cone is more or less egg-shaped and the seed capsules are very small and thin, scarcely protruding at all. Branches are densely coated with short, soft, matted fur, in which occasional long spreading hairs are often intermixed. The grey-green, rigid, leathery leaves are stalkless or almost so, oblong to rounded or heart-shaped, and bordered by small irregular prickly teeth. They are up to six centimetres long and are prominently veined underneath.

squat, scarlet and gold flowerheads of *B. coccinea* to the enormous pale yellow spikes of *B. grandis,* the bull banksia. The genus commemorates the name of Sir Joseph Banks, the botanist who accompanied Cook on his voyage of discovery and collected the first specimens in 1770 at Botany Bay.

There are about fifty species, all confined to Australia except one, *B. dentata,* which extends across tropical Australia to New Guinea. They are found in all States of the Commonwealth but occur most abundantly in Western Australia, where there are forty-odd endemic species. The vast majority of these are found in the southwest, that ancient corner of Australia which has remained segregated by sea and sand for countless millions of years, developing in isolation a unique and lovely flora.

Western banksias include some of the most fantastically decorative of the Proteaceae. They range from entirely prostrate shrubs such as *B. repens* and *B. prostrata,* which creep along underground with stems and even leaves often protectively buried beneath the surface of the southern sand plains so that the flower spikes appear to be squatting directly on the soil, to *B. grandis,* which grows to fifteen metres or more in the neighbouring coastal districts on the south-western tip of Australia, forming a spectacular understorey amid towering forests of jarrah and karri, and occurring in a stunted but profusely flowering form on the windswept hills overlooking the Southern Ocean. Enormous pale yellow flower spikes, up to forty-five centimetres long, are like great candles in the tree; branches are woolly-coated and the large shining dark green leaves are twenty-five centimetres or more long.

Another spectacular western species is the firewheel banksia, *B. menziesii,* which is closely allied to the eastern species, *B. serrata* and *B. serratifolia.* Flower spikes are short and squat, rarely more than ten to twelve centimetres long, and the silky, pink to rosy-red flowers bloom in autumn and winter.

Plate 15
ACORN BANKSIA—*Banksia prionotes*
The bright orange, prominent styles of this banksia are released from the bottom of the flower spike first, contrasting sharply with the soft, silvery-white buds and giving the inflorescence its acorn-like appearance. It grows as a tree, five to ten metres high, on white sand in several districts of the southwestern botanical province, ranging from King George Sound in the south to the Murchison River north of Geraldton. Spikes are up to fifteen centimetres long; the style is rigid, incurved at the base, then finally erect, with narrow furrowed stigma. Rounded seed capsules are prominent on the fruiting cones after the withered flowers have fallen. Bark of trunk and branches is ash-grey, softly and densely furred. Leaves are thirty centimetres or more long, about two centimetres broad, flat to undulate and regularly scalloped along the margins, each shallow lobe ending with a short rigid point. Numerous fine transverse veins, converging at the apex of each lobe, are clearly visible on the undersurface.

Plate 16
BAXTER'S BANKSIA—*Banksia baxteri*
The most striking feature of this banksia is the leaves, which are up to fourteen centimetres long and divided to the midrib into sharp-pointed triangular segments, the larger ones being up to three centimetres long and two centimetres broad at the base. The globular flower spikes are yellow, and about eight centimetres in diameter. Individual flowers, bracts and ends of branches bearing spikes are covered with long fine feather-like hairs, and seed capsules are thick and very prominent. This banksia grows as a tall, erect shrub two to three metres high, and is common around King George Sound and the flat sandy plains from the Stirling Range to the Pallinup River. It flowers in late spring and summer.

As with the eastern relatives, flower spikes in bud are silvery-grey, soft and velvety. In bloom they remain rose-pink or reddish while the looped tip of the wiry golden style remains firmly clasped between the perianth lobes; these styles are released from the bottom of the spike first, and finally the flower cone is transformed to a golden fuzz. *B. menziesii* is a tree, up to ten or twelve metres high and of rather straggling habit. Bark is pebbled and branches thickly woolly. Common in the Swan River district near Perth, its range extends northward to the Murchison River and the vicinity of Shark Bay, and inland across the sand plains of the Avon district.

The unusual round-fruit banksia, *B. spaerocarpa,* is widespread in the sandy heathlands of the southwest, from Albany to Geraldton, extending inland into the saltbush and mulga country of the Coolgardie district. A shrub a metre or so high, the spikes are globular or nearly so, mostly about five centimetres in diameter but sometimes almost twice as large. Flowers are usually bronze-yellow (violet-tinged in var. *violacea*) and they may be seen in bloom all year round, though most profusely in summer. Styles are much longer than the flowers and remain hooked, so that the inflorescence in full bloom looks like a golden pompom or exploding fireball on cracker night. The spherical fruiting cones are studded with rour ded seed capsules, each marked with a prominent ridge along the suture, or else enveloped in a mat of interwoven withered styles, looking for all the world like a bird's nest.

Branches are covered with minute blue-grey hairs, giving the bush a silvery sheen. Leaves are long and narrow, with margins tightly rolled back to the midrib and doubly grooved underneath. They vary in length from two to eight centimetres.

Leaves are the most remarkable feature of the showy banksia, *B. speciosa,* a tall spreading shrub of the sandy heathlands around Esperance. They spring from woolly white branches and are thirty centimetres or more long, divided to the midrib into numerous triangular lobes, like shark's teeth, the larger ones three centimetres broad at the base and almost as long, but diminishing in size towards the end of the leaf. These elongated leaves are flat and rigid, furry white underneath and marked with numerous transverse converging veins. Broad oblong flower spikes, twelve centimetres or so long, bloom in January. Perianths are hairy and yellowish-green, and the erect rigid styles are hairy also, and incurved at the base. This banksia was first recorded at Lucky Bay by Robert Brown, the young Scottish botanist who accompanied Flinders in *Investigator* during 1801-02. Over a period of three and a half years, Brown collected and described almost 4,000 species of Australian plants, the majority of them new to science.

Plate 17
ASHBY'S BANKSIA—*Banksia ashbyi*
This banksia usually occurs as a tall shrub or small tree, but may be stunted in growth and no more than a metre high. It is the typical banksia of the red sand country between Geraldton and Carnarvon; flowers are bright orange, and spikes squat, about eight centimetres broad and ten to twelve centimetres long. The long narrow leaves, two to three centimetres wide and up to twenty-five centimetres long, are deeply lobed, almost to the midrib. This banksia blooms in early spring.

Grevilleas, sometimes called spider flowers, form the largest genus of the family Proteaceae. They vary from prostrate trailing species to tall trees, but most are shrubby. With the exception of a few species in New Guinea, New Caledonia and the Celebes, they are entirely confined to Australia. There are over 200 endemic species and they are found in all parts of the continent, from tropical rainforests to the dry interior and from the islands of the north to Tasmania. By far the greatest number of species, however, are once again to be found in the southwest of Western Australia.

Flowers may be almost any colour except blue. They are arranged in loose racemes, short and radiating from the top of a common stalk in the typical 'spider flowers', such as G. wilsonii (Plate 18) and sometimes in long spikes such as G. leucopteris (Plate 19) or in one-sided, toothbrush-like sheaths, as in G. apiciloba, the black toothbrush grevillea of the sand heaths inland from Perth, and G. concinna, the red comb grevillea of southern sand plains. The style of Grevillea is long and slender, often hooked, and the floral tube usually splits down one side before the flower opens, allowing the style to protrude in a loop. This perianth tube may be straight, but is more often curved. As with other genera in the family, it is petaloid, and consists of four segments. Leaves are alternate and may vary greatly in shape and size. Some are tough and leathery, some silken soft; some entire, some divided and fern-like; others are sharp-pointed, toothed or prickly. Fruit is a small, often hairy, thin-shelled and brittle follicle, from which the style persists in a characteristic loop.

Two remarkable prostrate grevilleas of inland areas of the southwest are G. flexuosa and G. dryandroides. Rarely more than thirty centimetres high and perhaps twice as wide, G. flexuosa has long, much-divided leaves and resembles a tiny tangled monkey puzzle hung with long, loose racemes of dainty pale pink flowers. It grows in gravel and laterite country and blooms in late spring and early summer. G. dryandroides is the phalanx grevillea of sand heaths northeast of Perth, which trails its pink 'toothbrush' inflorescences across the bare earth during the hotter months of the year. A contrast is G. eriostachya, the flame grevillea of the northwest and arid interior. This spectacular grevillea is a pine-like shrub up to six metres tall, with long, large, bright orange flower spikes which blaze like beacons on the red sand ridges and spinifex country. It blooms profusely for many months, from early spring to late summer and its range extends southward to the region of salt Lake Barlee and as far inland as Ayers Rock in the Northern Territory. Individual flowers are large and clothed in fine silken hairs. They are arranged in crowded cone-like terminal racemes up to fifteen centimetres long. Leaves, fifteen to twenty centimetres long, are compound, consisting of three to five long, very narrow leaflets.

Plate 18
WILSON'S GREVILLEA—*Grevillea wilsonii*
This is one of the spider-flowered grevilleas, and is common in the jarrah forests of the southwest. It is a small shrub, dense and bushy, rarely much more than a metre in height. Vivid scarlet flowers are framed with finely divided, sharp-pointed leaves.

Plate 19
WHITE PLUMED GREVILLEA—*Grevillea leucopteris*
One of the most spectacular of western grevilleas is *G. leucopteris*, common on the northern sand plains and heathlands of Western Australia. An endemic species, it has large clusters of creamy flowers on long arching stems. A shrub, two to five metres high, it flowers in spring and summer, but unfortunately the flowers have a strong, unpleasant odour.

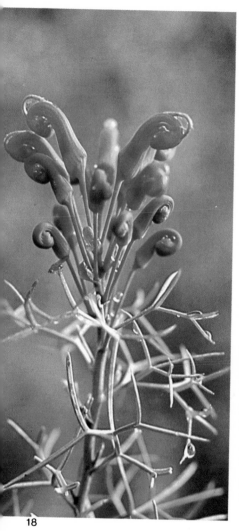

18

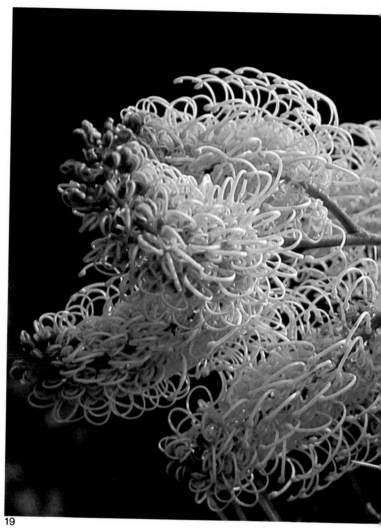

19

Dryandra is a large genus of the Proteaceae, comprising over sixty species, all of which are restricted to the southwest of Western Australia and some to a very limited section within that region. Dryandras have close links with the banksias. Flowers, usually various shades of yellow but in some species orange, red, pink or even purple, are massed into round heads within a circle of persistent bracts (in *Banksia* they are arranged in a spiral around a spike). In some *Dryandra* species the characteristic encircling bracts are conspicuous and colourful, and form the most attractive portion of the inflorescence. The group as a whole has most decorative foliage; leaves are nearly always serrated, often grouped in a ring around the flowerheads, and vary greatly in length, width and pattern. In many species they are long and narrow, in others they are short, broad and holly-like.

Height and habit are also variable, ranging from prostrate shrubs to small trees.

Perhaps the most dramatic of the dryandras, with flowerheads eight to ten centimetres long, is the king dryandra, *D. proteoides*. Massed golden flowers are surrounded by prominent, orange-red bracts, and the prickly, lobed leaves are up to twenty centimetres long. A shrub up to two metres tall, it grows on ironstone ridges in a limited area to the east of Perth. One of the tallest is *D. arborea,* a small tree up to six metres tall with pale yellow flowerheads five centimetres across and rigid, prickly leaves. In contrast, *D. obtusa,* the shining honeypot, is a prostrate shrub with underground stems, so that only the bright flowers and rigid, divided leaves up to thirty centimetres long, are visible, and appear as if they are just sitting on the ground.

Xylomelum is a genus of four species, all confined to Australia—two in the east and two in the west. These are the woody pears, remarkable for their large pear-shaped wooden fruit, up to ten centimetres long, which splits along the upper side to reveal two flat winged seeds. Leaves are leathery, conspicuously veined, and may be entire or finely serrated along the margin. Flowers are carried in dense spikes in the leaf axils. The two western species are *X. angustifolium,* the sand plain pear, a shrub or small tree up to seven metres tall, common on the sand plains north of Perth, with narrow entire leaves and silvery-grey fruits, and *X. occidentale,* a slightly larger tree common in the jarrah forests further south, which has large, rusty brown fruits and broad holly-like leaves. Both bear masses of creamy white blossoms in mid-summer.

In startling contrast to the massive, woody and completely inedible 'pears' of *Xylomelum* is the fruit of *Persoonia,* another genus of the family. This is a succulent, fleshy drupe, in many species edible—the 'jibbongs' of the Aboriginals, who sought them for food; many are still popularly called geebungs. The group is confined to Australia, except for one species which extends to New Zealand, and there are about seventy species, occurring in all States, with about twenty-seven in the southwest of Western Australia.

Plate 20
URCHIN DRYANDRA—*Dryandra praemorsa*
This dryandra has large yellow flowerheads with prominent styles up to five centimetres long, and oak-like leaves up to ten centimetres in length. An attractive bushy shrub which grows from one to three metres tall among granite rocks of the Darling district·east of Perth, it is winter-flowering.

Adenanthos is an Australian genus of twenty species of shrubs, all confined to the southwest of Western Australia except two, one of which extends to South Australia and the other being restricted to the mallee country of that State and western Victoria. Popularly called jug or basket flowers, *Adenanthos* is closely related to *Grevillea*, differing mainly in that flowers are solitary, and not in clusters or spikes. They are usually red or rarely greenish in colour, with small bracts at the base and long arched styles protruding characteristically from a slit in the corolla tube. Foliage is often very attractive, in some species being the most decorative feature of the plant.

Hakeas are a group of over 130 species of shrubs and trees, all endemic to Australia and most confined to the west, where there are about eighty species. Individual flowers are carried on short stems in axillary clusters or racemes along the branches. The slender floral tube splits along one side while still in bud, allowing the style to protrude in a loop; later the petal segments roll back and usually become free. Fruit is a large, very thick, hard woody capsule, two-valved and often rounded, with a beak-like projection. Seeds are winged. Leaves are alternate and, like those of other members of the family Proteaceae, show considerable variation. In many species they are much reduced, cylindrical and sharp-pointed— hakeas are commonly called needlebushes because of this—but in others they may be flat, entire, serrated or divided. Several western species have flowers clustered into rounded heads topped by long, conspicuous yellow styles, the whole resembling a bright sea urchin or colourful pincushion crowned with golden pins. Both names are commonly applied to them. One such is the pincushion hakea, *H. laurina,* a native of the sand

24

Plate 21
WOOLLYBUSH—*Adenanthos cygnorum*
Tallest in the genus, this is a common shrub around Perth, where it can be seen growing in sandy soils to a height of about four metres. Its most attractive feature is the grey-green foliage, which is red-tipped when new. The pale, greenish flowers are inconspicuous among the leaves.

Plate 22
BASKET FLOWER—*Adenanthos obovatus*
A slender many-stemmed shrub up to about a metre in height, *A. obovatus* is found in sandy and swampy areas from around Albany to just north of Perth. Throughout the winter months it bears attractive, bright scarlet flowers, cupped in the axils of rounded, slightly recurved leaves. The tubular flowers are up to two centimetres long and the styles protrude at least as far again.

plains of the southwest which grows as a large shrub or small tree to four metres in height and bears densely crowded, ball-type flowers up to five centimetres across, during autumn and winter.

Another is the sea urchin hakea, *H. petiolaris,* a tall shrub to five metres which is also winter-blooming. A western hakea with long, bottlebrush type flowerheads is *H. bucculenta,* the 'red pokers' common in the tall scrub north of the Murchison River. The showy flower spikes, combined with long, fine, grass-like foliage, make this handsome shrub one of the most spectacular in the genus. It grows to about three metres and flowers in August.

Another attractive and most unusual hakea is *H. cucullata,* commonly called scallops, a reference to the large broad cupped leaves which support and frame the racemes of clustered pink flowers. It grows to about three metres and is common in the Stirling Ranges.

Two closely related genera of the family Proteaceae are both commonly known as drumsticks or conebushes. These are *Isopogon* and *Petrophile*. In both, numerous flowers are crowded in dense cylindrical formations around a woolly stem, each individual bloom being protected by a scale-like bract. These bracts overlap one another and become enlarged as the flowers fade, so that the heads resemble a pinecone in appearance. In *Isopogon* this cone is round and woolly; the fruit, a small hairy nut, is embedded in the scales and falls off with them. In *Petrophile* the cone is elongated and the bracts remain persistent, in time opening out to allow the small nutlets to shake loose. There are over thirty species of *Isopogon,* and about forty of *Petrophile*. Both genera are restricted to Australia, their greatest development being in the west.

Twenty-five *Isopogon* species are endemic to the west, shrubs varying in height from thirty centimetres to three or four metres and in colour from pale cream to deep pink. *Isopogon latifolius,* a tall shrub of the Stirling Range, is probably the most magnificent, with bright pink to purple flowers up to eight centimetres across, the largest of the genus. A common *Isopogon* of gravelly soils in the Darling Range is *I. sphaerocephalus,* the roundheaded drumstick, which grows one to two metres in height and carries bright yellow flowerheads up to four centimetres across.

Plate 23
BARREL CONEFLOWER—*Isopogon triblobus*
An upright, leafy shrub, fairly dense and about a metre in height, this *Isopogon* grows on the southern sand plains and has most interesting foliage. Leaves are fan-shaped, up to seven centimetres long, and divided at the end into broad, sharp-pointed lobes, usually three in number but sometimes more. Flowerheads are bright yellow and numerous, about three centimetres long and the same across, and the globular grey fruiting cone is a little smaller.

Plate 24
A HAKEA—*Hakea amplexifolia*
Main interest in this hakea centres on the large stem-clasping prickly leaves, fifteen to twenty centimetres long and broadest at the deeply lobed base. New growth and margins of young leaves are rusty red. Flowers, white tinged with pink, are carried in the leaf axils in September. This is an upright shrub of the southwest forest country which grows to two metres or so in height.

23

There are about thirty Western Australian species of *Petrophile*, all confined to the southwest corner of the State. Colours range from almost white through cream and yellow to various shades of pink. *P. divaricata* is an inland species of the plains and ridges. It has attractive, bright yellow flowerheads up to three centimetres across and unusual, much-divided, very prickly foliage, grows to about a metre in height and flowers in spring. *P. biloba* is the granite petrophile, restricted to the Darling Range east of Perth. Its flowers are a soft grey-pink, and are carried in profuse leafy spikes in late winter.

The flowers of *Conospermum*, another mainly western genus of the Proteaceae, are usually woolly, greyish-blue in colour, and carried like a smoky cloud in massed plumes above the foliage. This has inspired the vernacular name, smokebush, though in some species the flowers are pure white, bright blue, lilac or pink, and may be glabrous. Leaves are always stiff, alternate, and entire, varying in shape from long and broad to small, crowded and heath-like. Flowers are stalkless, and contained within a broad, persistent, usually hairy bract. As with all Proteaceae the floral parts are in fours, but in *Conospermum* the four tiny lobes of the floral tube are unequal, the rear one being much larger than the others. Fruit is a small hairy conical nut, tufted at the top. There are about fifty species, the vast majority confined to the southwest of Western Australia though representatives are to be found in all States. Two western species which do not conform to the typical 'smokebush' pattern are *C. caeruleum* and *C. brownii*, neither of which have the familiar woolly flowers and neither of which are grey. In *C. caeruleum* they are deep blue, and in *C. brownii*, the blue-eyed smokebush, white flowers surround unopened buds of cobalt blue, giving the inflorescence a wide-eyed effect.

28

Plate 25
SLENDER SMOKEBUSH—*Conospermum huegelii*
Flowers of the slender smokebush are carried on long stems arising from a tuft of narrow, curly basal leaves. It grows in damp situations on the eastern coastal plain and Darling Range. Flowers, considerably enlarged in this picture, are up to one centimetre long; they vary in colour from smoky-grey to blue, and are carried in winter and spring.

Plate 26
PIXIE MOPS—*Petrophile linearis*
This *Petrophile* inhabits the sandy coastal stretches from the Hill River to south of Perth. A small shrub, less than a metre in height, it has soft woolly pink flowers, tipped with grey, and carried in crowded heads up to five centimetres across. It blooms in spring. The narrow pointed leaves are curved.

26

25

Family LORANTHACEAE

The Mistletoes

Mistletoes are semi-parasitic, attaching themselves to branches or, rarely, roots of other plants, and drawing water and mineral nutrients from the host.

All, however, have green leaves and manufacture their own food by photosynthesis. There are about a dozen Australian genera, embracing over sixty species. Five genera and over twenty species occur in Western Australia, including the endemic, monotypic genus *Nuytsia,* the single species of which is the most spectacular Western Australian Christmas tree, *N. floribunda,* which grows as a tree attached to the roots of the host, rather than as a many-branched shrub attached to the limbs of trees, as do most of the family.

Conventional epiphytic mistletoes can also be seen hanging in pendulous fashion from branches in the Australian bush. These are all indigenous. In many cases each species attaches itself chiefly to a particular genus of host tree—eucalypts, acacias, casuarinas, grevilleas—and sometimes they seem to mimic the foliage of the host. Flowers are often brightly coloured and a source of nectar for honey-sucking birds, and the succulent, berry-like fruit, vivid scarlet or glowing orange, are an important food source for other birds, some species being entirely dependent on them. *Amyema,* with over thirty species, the majority of them endemic, is the largest Australian genus. Sixteen occur in Western Australia, including *A. fitzgeraldii,* the pincushion mistletoe, which occurs only on *Acacia* species and has succulent, red, hoary fruit. Flowerheads are green and red, the long perianth splitting to the base while the red stamens and style remain erect.

Plate 27
WESTERN AUSTRALIAN CHRISTMAS TREE—
Nuytsia floribunda
In December this remarkable tree blazes with glorious colour. Orange-gold flowers, sweetly honey-scented, are carried in racemes up to a foot long and almost completely obscure the foliage. Though a member of the mistletoe family and semi-parasitic, it grows as a stout-trunked tree, anything up to ten metres high and often in apparent isolation. It secures water and certain nutrients by tapping the roots of neighbouring plants and, while its favoured host appears to be *Banksia* species, it has been known to grow in association with much smaller plants, such as grass. It is a native of the southwest, where it is also known as the Swan River blaze tree. Leaves are thick and narrow, up to eight centimetres long. Branches are brittle and the wood soft and spongy.

27

Family SANTALACEAE

The Sandalwoods

This family includes the fragrant white sandalwood of the Orient, *Santalum alba,* much prized and sought after for centuries by adventurers from many lands, and the Australian quandong, *S. acuminatum,* with its bright red, edible, stony-hearted fruit. It is closely related to the mistletoes and, like them, parasitic, but whereas the latter, with the notable exception of *Nuytsia floribunda,* occur as parasites on the branches of trees, members of the Santalaceae are shrubs or trees, with roots in the soil but deriving some of their nourishment from the roots of neighbouring plants by means of sucker-like attachments. Flowers are small and insignificant, but the fruit, which is a nut, drupe or berry, is often brightly coloured and succulent. Leaves are entire, opposite or alternate, and in some species are reduced to minute scales so that the plant appears to be leafless.

There are eight Australian species of *Santalum,* two of them—both from the west—being valuable timber trees and once the basis of an extensive export trade in sandalwood. *Santalum spicatum,* the fragrant or Swan River sandalwood, is confined to the south of Western Australia and some sections of South Australia. Timber is a source of high quality sandalwood oil, used for perfumes and incense. Farther north is *S. lanceolatum,* a slender tree also valued for its timber; its small, edible, dark purple fruit were a food source for Aboriginals.

There are also a number of *Exocarpos* species in Western Australia. These endemic Australian members of the Santalaceae are the native cherries, fruit of which is a small hard nut borne at the end of a fleshy, succulent, bright red or orange stalk, so that it looks like a cherry turned inside out. Flowers are minute, and true leaves are scale-like, their function performed by slender cypress-like branches.

Plate 28
QUANDONG—*Santalum acuminatum*
An attractive tall shrub or small tree, this is the sweet quandong, fruit of which is a bright red, globular drupe with a succulent but thin outer layer of flesh covering a large and very hard, wrinkled and pitted stone. The flesh is edible and can be used for jams and preserves while the decorative nuts have been used for beads, ornaments and as counters in games such as Chinese checkers. The quandong occurs in all States and in Western Australia is common in the south and inland areas generally. It is a graceful tree, with drooping habit and lance-shaped, dull green leaves five to eight centimetres long. Flowers are tiny, creamy-white and carried in sprays about as long as the leaves. Another species, smaller, and with narrower, silvery leaves, is *S. murrayanum,* the bitter quandong, which has a similar range but, as the common name implies, bears bitter-tasting fruit.

Family CHENOPODIACEAE

The Saltbushes

This very large, world-wide family of salt-tolerant, often succulent plants is well represented in the arid salt lake region of the central south of Western Australia and is the dominant vegetation in the salty sea marshes and sand dunes of the coast. Many genera, particularly *Atriplex,* are commonly called saltbushes, an allusion not only to the salty nature of their habitat but also to the saline content of their foliage; indeed, some species absorb salt to such an extent that they can be used in the reclamation of alkaline soils, gradually lowering the salt concentration until the level is acceptable to other forms of plant life. The drought-resistant saltbushes are also most valuable fodder plants, providing year-round pasture for sheep in near-arid areas.

Atriplex has separate male and female flowers, both usually inconspicuous, and a curious fruiting structure consisting of two fused flaps, often colourful and sometimes swollen and spongy, with a single seed embedded at the base. *Kochia,* another genus of the family common to warm temperate regions but with its richest development in Australia, is also well represented in dry inland areas of the west. Australian species are commonly known as bluebushes, a reference to their bluish grey, downy foliage. Once again there is a strange wing-like expansion of the fruit rim, often brightly coloured. They are useful fodder plants, like most members of the family. In *Enchylaena,* an endemic Australian genus, the whole flower becomes swollen, succulent and berry-like. Other chenopods found in the west are known as the berry saltbushes, and belong to the mainly Australian genus, *Rhagodia,* which includes the fragrant saltbush, *R.*

parabolica, leaves of which were used by early settlers as a green vegetable (after boiling to remove some of the salt) and the red-fruited sea-berry saltbush, *R. baccata,* which colonises the sand dunes up and down the Western Australian coast. The succulent-stemmed samphires, of the genera *Arthrocnemum, Teticornia* and *Salicornia,* are strange leafless plants with jointed stems composed of green fleshy cylindrical sections, the uppermost joints of which form the spike for the insignificant flowers. They flourish in coastal salt marshes and inland claypans. Aboriginal tribes sought them for food.

Plate 29
A BLUEBUSH—*Maireana carnosa* (syn. *Kochia carnosa*)
This is a brittle undershrub with hoary foliage and flowers hidden within a mass of long soft hairs, which form a loose tawny woollen ball one centimetre or more in diameter. It is a plant of the salt flats and sandy plains of the Eremean province and grows to about thirty centimetres.

Plate 30
RUBY SALTBUSH—*Enchyleana tomentosa*
The berry-like 'fruits' of this saltbush are actually the flattened, succulent flowers. It occurs in northern and central areas of Western Australia and is common throughout inland Australia generally. It is a low, sprawling shrub with densely-haired cylindrical leaves, and is a valuable fodder plant.

Family AMARANTHACEAE

The Amaranths

The plants of this family are small shrubs or herbs, occasionally climbers, with simple, entire leaves. Flowers are usually stalkless within dry papery bracts, and in most genera they are carried in dense, congested heads. The family is widespread in tropical and subtropical regions of the world and includes garden favourites such as love-lies-bleeding (*Amaranthus caudatus*), cockscomb (*Celosia cristata*) and bachelor's buttons (*Gomphrena* species). Several genera are represented in Western Australia (including *Amaranthus* and *Gomphrena*) but the great majority of indigenous species belong to the wholly Australian genus, *Ptilotus*. There are over 100 *Ptilotus* species, (including those formerly classified as *Trichonium* —the two genera have now been united) and they are herbs or small shrubs of the hot dry regions.

Leaves are alternate, and often hairy. The papery flowers, sometimes brightly coloured, are covered with soft, feathery hairs and borne in densely packed terminal heads or spikes. The Aboriginals called them 'mullamulla', early settlers 'lambstails' or 'featherheads', and all three names are still in common use.

There is considerable variation within this genus. Some are ephemeral annuals which carpet the arid inland areas after the rains; they germinate, flower, set seed and die, all within a few short weeks, then lie dormant as seeds during the dry period. Others are robust perennial shrubs which grow to a metre or more in height. Flowers of *Ptilotus* may be massed in dense globular heads or carried in long cylindrical spikes, perhaps thirty centimetres or more in length, and they occur in various shades of pink, purple, yellow, white or even green. Leaves in some species are smooth and form a basal rosette; in others, the shrubby types, they occur up the stems and may be hairy or grey-felted.

Plate 31
MULLAMULLA—*Ptilotus macrocephalus*
The rounded fluffy flowerheads of this mullamulla are up to eight centimetres across. They are a shining white or pale honey colour, tinged with green and tipped with gold, and sometimes form large cylindrical spikes up to twenty centimetres long. Leaves are long and narrow, and chiefly at the ground. Flowerheads are carried on slender stems which may be almost a metre in length.

Family AIZOACEAE

The Noon-flowers

The Aizoaceae is a mainly South African family, and includes the little garden succulents commonly called pigface, and the livingstone daisies. About a dozen genera occur in Australia, including *Carpobrotus,* a mostly South African genus, and *Disphyma,* a monotypic Australian genus, the single species of which is *D. australe.* These little native succulents have prostrate stems which root from the nodes, enabling the plants to subdue shifting sand, and thick fleshy leaves which store water, so that they can survive in arid conditions. The two genera are closely allied, differing mainly in that flowers of *Disphyma* are stalked and the mature fruit is a dry capsule, whereas the fruit of *Carpobrotus* is a succulent, edible berry. They grow in saline soil of sea marshes and inland saltpans, clambering over sand dunes and wave-splashed rocks and carpeting great areas of the interior around the dry salt lakes. An interesting fact about these flowers is that there are no true petals. The shining colourful ring of soft fine filaments consists of flattened, petal-like, undeveloped stamens. These surround the inner circle of fertile stamens, opening widely in bright sunlight and closing at night or in dull weather (hence the common name, 'noon-flowers').

Family RANUNCULACEAE

The Buttercups

Western Australian members of this family include several species of *Ranunculus*, the yellow buttercups of damp places, two of *Clematis*, the starry-flowered 'travellers' joy which grows chiefly near water, and one of *Myosurus*, *M. minimus*, the curious little mousetail, a dwarf ephemeral of the dry inland, where it is found in areas subject to periodic flooding. The family derives its name from the Latin *ranunculus*—'little frog'—an allusion to the preference most members have for damp places. It has a wide distribution in cool and temperate regions of the world, being particularly abundant in the northern hemisphere, and includes many lovely garden flowers—larkspur, delphinium, columbine, love-in-a-mist, anemone and peony. Members are herbs or climbers, the herbaceous types having leaves alternate or in a rosette at the base.

Plate 32

A PIGFACE—*Carpobrotus* species
The various native species of *Carpobrotus* are mainly plants of the seashore, found on coastal dunes and rocky foreshores. They are prostrate plants with long, triangular, fleshy leaves and short, erect flowering branches. Fruits are juicy and edible, though somewhat salty, and were sought after by Aboriginals for food. Flowers are up to eight centimetres in diameter, and occur in various shades of pink and yellow.

Plate 33

A CLEMATIS—*Clematis pubescens*
Clematis species often grow near water, thereby earning the vernacular name, 'travellers' joy'. They are woody climbers which ramble over shrubs, fallen logs and creek banks, clinging by means of modified leaf stalks. *C. pubescens* is the common clematis of southwest coastal areas and the jarrah forests. Flowers have no petals, but four pure white, petal-like sepals. Stamens are numerous, and also carpels, the styles of which persist in long feathery plumes on the tightly clustered fruit, rather like a hoary beard, and inspiring the alternative common name, 'old man's beard'.

32

33

Family CEPHALOTACEAE

The Pitcher-plant

This family has only one member, the strange, carnivorous Western Australian pitcher-plant, *Cephalotus follicularis*, which traps insects in jug-like receptacles and digests them in juices which it secretes. Endemic to the Albany region of the southwest of Western Australia, it is found in moist swampy areas and bears two different kinds of leaves—normal foliage leaves, which are flat, green and rather fleshy, and the greatly modified, jug-like 'pitchers' formed from the leaf stalk and topped by a small, lid-like, partially translucent true leaf. These pitchers start to develop in early spring and are bright green when young; as they grow, they change in colour, becoming red-veined in the upper portion and finally purple in the lower. Full grown specimens may be five centimetres deep and three centimetres broad at the base; three strong, girder-like vertical ridges—the centre one extending almost from the base to the orifice—are equipped with stiff, ladder-like bristles, which are believed to assist the progress of crawling insects into the trap.

The translucent, half-open lid acts as a lure and landing platform for flying insects. Whatever the method of arrival, once the insect visitors reach the smooth slippery mouth of the trap, they slide into the internal cavity, with its nectar-baited acid solution in which the majority quickly drown. Three barriers prevent the escape of any who manage to struggle free—the smooth concave nature of the inner surface, a downward-pointing ledge which projects from the inner rim and a palisade of sharp teeth which curve around the lip into the cavity. These plants grow in clumps, several springing from the one underground stem which branches and produces many clusters of leaves on the surface. As indicated, the flamboyant pitchers are modified leaves, but the plant does produce true flowers: small, white and sweetly perfumed, they are carried in panicles on long stems in late summer.

Plate 34
WESTERN AUSTRALIAN PITCHER-PLANT—
Cephalotus follicularis
The colourful insect-trapping pitchers of this carnivorous plant are modified leaves; the true flowers are small, with six white petals, borne in loose panicles on very long stems. Also known as the Albany pitcher-plant, it occurs only in the extreme southwest of Western Australia, in swampy areas around Albany.

Family MIMOSACEAE

The Wattles

The wattle family consists of about forty genera and over 2,500 species of shrubs and trees, widely dispersed in tropical, subtropical and temperate parts of the world, particularly Africa, South America and Australia. The family name comes from the genus *Mimosa*, so called because the leaves of many species mimic animal movements, drooping and closing at the touch of a finger, responding to darkness and light: the 'sensitive plants' of European hot-houses.

Australia has no true mimosas; here the family is represented mainly by *Acacia* species—wattles—though there are a few other genera, including the closely related *Albizia* (the western *Albizia lophantha* is sometimes called the Cape Leeuwin wattle) and *Neptunia* (*Neptunia gracilis* is the native sensitive plant of the Kimberleys). Australia, however, is the main home of the acacias; there are over 650 indigenous species, all but a few of them confined to this continent and more than half of them to the west. They form the largest genus in the flora of the land and are the most widespread of all Australian plants. In the west they range from the feathery-leaved species of the cool depths of jarrah and karri forests to the jam trees and mulgas of the parched interior, which, like the majority of Australian wattles, are leafless in the true sense.

Wattles fall into two broad categories: those that retain true leaves (always bipinnate, or fern-like) and those with leaves reduced to phyllodes (flattened stalks performing the function of leaves). These leaf-like modified stalks are tougher than true leaves and appear better able to withstand the arid conditions of many parts of Australia. They occur in an infinite variety of shapes and sizes: stiff and spine-like, elongated or reduced to mere prickles, broad, sickle-shaped, rounded or needle-like. All phyllodinous wattles, however, have this factor in common: seedling leaves are always bipinnate. As the plants grow, the true leaves are reduced to phyllodes and it is not uncommon, in young plants, to see the phyllode developing at the base of the compound leaf.

Plate 35

A WATTLE—*Acacia cuneata*
This glorious little wattle is capable of growing in the most exposed and barren situations, in almost pure sand on rocky, windswept sea coast and semi-arid areas. A low spreading shrub rarely higher than about fifty centimetres, it blooms in late winter and spring, carrying masses of deep yellow fluffy flowerballs which are borne singly in the axils. The specific name, *cuneata*, refers to the phyllodes, which are an inverted wedge shape, with a single central vein. It is confined to the southwest.

Plate 36

WINGED WATTLE—*Acacia alata*
Phyllodes are reduced to mere prickles in this unusual leafless wattle and flattened winged stems up to three centimetres wide perform the function of leaves. It is a low-growing shrub, confined to the southwest corner of the continent and usually found in moist shady situations. Large, fluffy, pale yellow flowerballs up to one centimetre across appear along the bare stems in winter and early spring, and the flat curved pods are hairy, with thick margins.

Plate 37

KARRI WATTLE—*Acacia pentadenia*
The karri wattle is a tall shrub, up to five metres in height, which grows in association with karri gums in the extreme southwest corner of Australia. The flowering season is from July to December, and the flowerheads are clustered in the axils of the long, bipinnate leaves. This is one of the few Western Australian acacias with true leaves, rather than the flattened modified leaf stalks or phyllodes of most species.

36

35

37

Family FABACEAE
(formerly Papilionaceae)

The Pea-flowers

These are the leguminous plants with typical 'pea' flowers, as distinct from the other pod-bearers, the Mimosaceae and the Caesalpiniaceae. Flowers always have five petals. The upper one, erect and usually large, is called the standard; it overlaps the others and encloses them in bud. With the two lateral (side) petals, it forms the characteristic butterfly wings which inspired the former family name (Papilionaceae, from the Latin, *papilio*, butterfly). The two lower petals are united into a wedge-like keel.

The standard varies in shape and size. In *Clianthus* (Sturt's desert pea, Plate 38) it is large, elongated and pointed. In others, such as *Hovea* (Plate 40) it is almost circular. In *Brachysema*, an almost exclusively Western Australian genus, it is small and inconspicuous, and the keel with its close-fitting wings is most prominent, giving the impression that the flower is not fully open (Plates 44 and 46).

Another distinguishing factor is the stamens. Always ten in number, they are either all free, all united into a tube, or nine united and one free. Leaves may be simple or compound, often trifoliate (simple leaves in threes on the one stem) or pinnate (compound leaves with leaflets arranged on opposite sides of a common leaf stalk). In some species leaves end in a tendril.

The pea family is a large one, widespread throughout the world, and a valuable one economically. It includes vegetables such as peas and beans and fodder crops such as lucerne. Peanuts belong to it, as do many lovely garden plants—lupin, broom, sweet pea and wisteria. The family also embraces many valuable timber trees, including the Australian black bean, *Castanospermum australe*, a tall rainforest tree of the eastern coast.

Plate 38
STURT'S DESERT PEA—*Clianthus formosus*
With its vivid red petals and glossy black central boss, Sturt's desert pea is one of the most spectacular of all Australian plants. Individual blooms are up to ten centimetres long and hang in clusters at the top of short erect stems. The standard is large and reflexed, and the keel of equal length, while the wings are small and much shorter. Stamens are united into a tube, with the exception of the upper one, which is free. Leaves are pinnate with up to seven pairs of large, oval leaflets, and foliage is densely coated with silky, silvery-grey hairs. There are two forms: one, common in the Kalgoorlie region, is a prostrate runner with stems lying on the ground and forming a mat covering several square metres from a single plant; the other, which seems to occur only in the Hamersley Range/Port Hedland district of Western Australia, is semi-erect. This form almost always has a dark red, rather than a shiny black, boss on the standard.

Sturt's desert pea occurs naturally in the arid inland, extending from Kalgoorlie to the Kimberleys, the offshore islands of the Dampier Archipelago and across the continent to the western plains of Queensland and New South Wales. The first specimens were gathered on the northwest coast by Dampier in 1699, and it owes its common name to the explorer Charles Sturt who collected samples during his journey to Cooper Creek in 1844. The generic name, *Clianthus*, is aptly chosen; it is from the Greek *kleos*, glory, and *anthos*, flower. There are only two species in the genus: Sturt's desert pea, confined to Australia, and the red kowhai or parrot's beak (*C. puniceus*) an ornamental small shrub native to New Zealand.

In Western Australia, however, family members are more noted as a stock hazard than as fodder, for a number of indigenous species are pea-flowered poisons, such as *Isotropis cunefolia*, the dainty 'granny's bonnet', otherwise known as lamb poison, with its widespread, bonnet-shaped flowers of yellow and pink, prettily purple-streaked behind, which are carried singly on slender stems.

There are over fifty genera and about 500 species of the pea-flowered Fabaceae in the west. *Spaerolobium* (Plate 39) is a genus of about a dozen or so species of small erect shrubs, usually leafless and mostly confined to the southwest corner of the State. Flowers are usually red or orange, with a yellow base, and are produced along the stems in dense spike-like racemes. Fruit, a small round pod, is the origin of the common name, 'globe pea'. Another chiefly western genus of leafless, or almost leafless, shrubs is *Jacksonia* (Plate 42). Quite a few of these stiff little shrubs or small trees have a strong odour, which has inspired the common name of 'stinkwood'. The typical pea-flowers of yellow, orange and red are borne along the stems or carried in racemes. Leaves are reduced to spines, and their function is taken over by flattened stems, sometimes with flowers on their margins.

The majority of Australian pea-flowers are in shades of yellow, orange, red or brown. Exceptions include *Hovea* and *Hardenbergia*; their flowers are intense blues and purples, though *Hardenbergia* does also occur in pink and white-flowered forms. *Hovea* is a wholly Australian genus, with about twelve species, six of which are confined to the south of Western Australia. In this genus the typical peaflowers are carried either in short racemes or in clusters in the leaf axils. The standard petal is almost circular and notched at the centre. Stamens are united and fruit is a globular or oval inflated pod.

Hoveas are shrubs or undershrubs; largest of the western species is *H. elliptica*, the tree hovea (Plate 40) which grows as high as three metres. Many species have prickly foliage, such as *H. pungens*, commonly called 'devil's pins', an erect shrub, up to two metres, with narrow, sharply pointed leaves. Another prickly hovea is *H. acanthoclada*, known as the thorny hovea, a rigid spreading shrub up to a metre or so high, which has deep purple flowers and grows as far inland as Kalgoorlie.

Plate 39
A GLOBE PEA—*Spaerolobium macranthum*
This globe pea is a small erect plant, seldom more than about thirty centimetres high, which bears large numbers of small red flowers on slender leafless stems in spring. It grows in the jarrah country of the southwest.

Plate 40
TREE HOVEA—*Hovea elliptica*
Also known as the karri bluebush, this hovea grows only in the karri and jarrah forests of the southwest. Leaves are elliptical to lance-shaped and stems and branches are rusty-woolly. The deep blue flowers are borne in axillary racemes in spring.

40

39

Hardenbergia is also a wholly Australian genus, with three species, one of which is confined to the west. These are twining plants, which occasionally grow upright. They are usually purple-flowered and are commonly known as native wisteria or false sarsaparilla. Leaves are long and lance-shaped, and resemble those of sarsaparilla (*Smilax* species), hence the alternate common name. The western species, *H. comptoniana,* is a vigorous climber which bears great trusses of small, violet-blue flowers in winter and spring, carpeting the forest floor and clambering over shrubs and fallen logs in the karri and jarrah country of the southwest.

Other twining members of the Fabaceae belong to the genus *Kennedia,* known as the coral peas. There are about sixteen species in this Australian genus, most of them endemic in the southwest of Western Australia. They are relatively large-flowered and include the vivid scarlet *K. prostrata,* known as running postman, and the black and yellow *K. nigricans,* the black cockatoo flower. Another trailing pea plant is *Abrus,* of which Australia has only one species, *A. precatorius,* noted for its bright scarlet, black-blotched, hard and shining seeds which are commonly called jequerity beans. This straggling climber on large trees extends across the tropical north of Australia but is not confined to this continent, occurring also in other tropical areas of the world.

Gompholobium is a genus of about twenty-five species, all confined to Australia and commonly known as wedge peas from the characteristic shape of the flowerbuds. Members are found in all States; Western Australia has sixteen, all endemic. The wedge peas are small erect shrubs. Leaves are alternate and often in sets of three leaflets branching from a common base, like the fingers of a hand. Flowers are usually large and, with the exception of one blue-flowered and one purple-flowered

Western Australian species, they are all yellow to orange-red in colour. Stamens are free and the keel sometimes has a fringe of fine hairs. Pods are inflated and round, or nearly so.

The largest Australian genus of pea-flowered plants is *Pultenaea,* with over 100 species, about thirty of which are to be found in Western Australia. These are the bush peas, a group entirely confined to this continent and well-represented in all States and a variety of habitats. They grow in coastal sand dunes and on the mountain tops, in peaty swamps and on the dry sand plains of the inland. They vary in habit from prostrate mat-like plants to large shrubs. Western species range from *Pultenaea arida,* a diffuse, yellow-flowered shrub, twenty-five to thirty centimetres high, found on the arid saltpans of the interior, to *P. pinifolia,* a tall shrub with needle-like foliage which grows to a height of three metres in wet sand in the extreme southwest corner of the State.

Plate 41
A WEDGE PEA—*Gompholobium ovatum*
A small shrub, twenty-five to forty centimetres high, this wedge pea grows in the Albany area of the southwest and flowers in October.

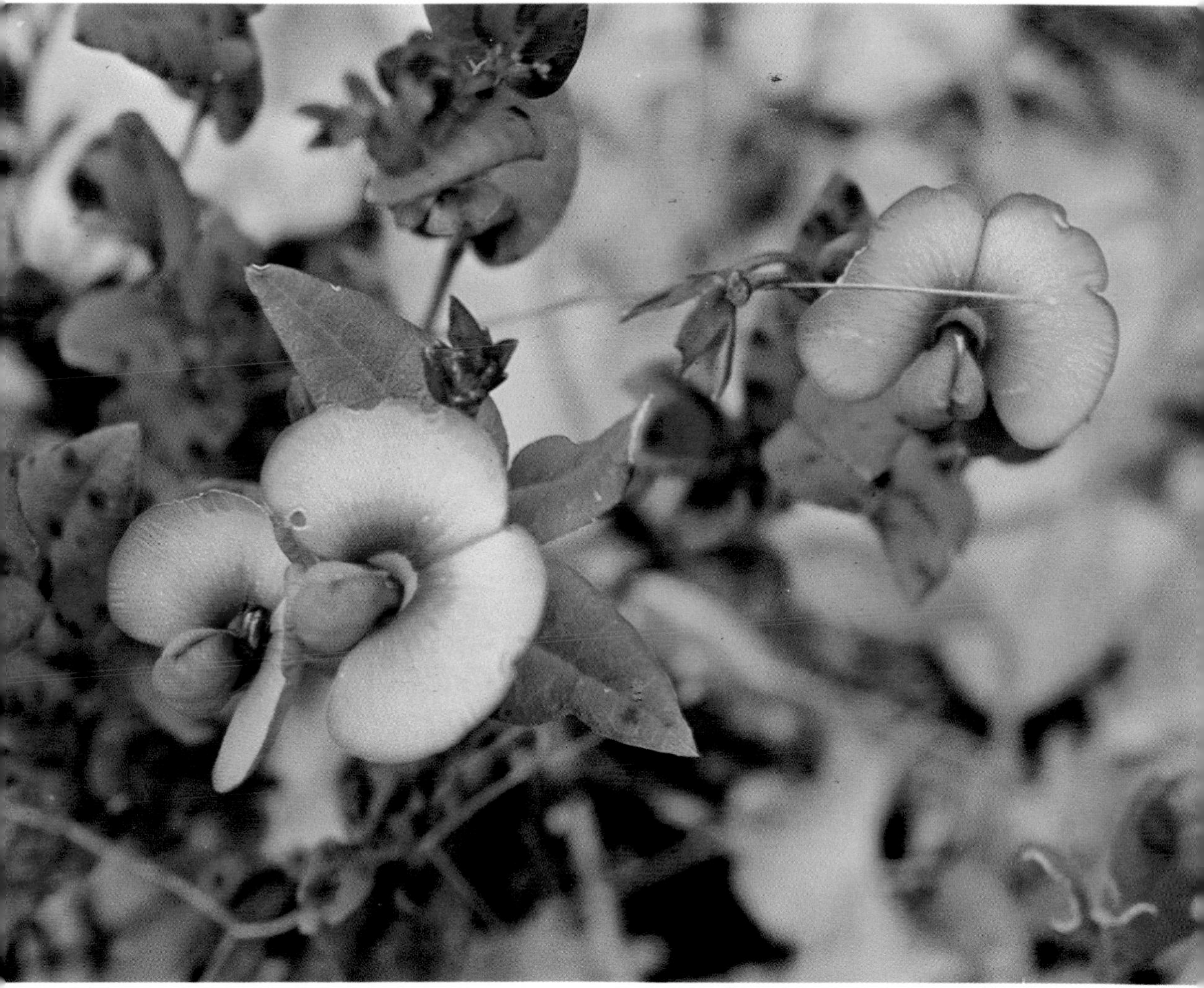

The genus *Chorizema* consists of eighteen species of shrubs and twining plants, all except one confined to Western Australia. It was first described by botanist Labillardière who, as a member of Bruny D'Entrecasteaux's expedition in 1792, collected the first specimens near Esperance Bay. It has been said that the delightful generic name is derived from *choros,* dance, and *zema,* a drinking vessel, and was chosen because he and his party danced for joy when they found the plant growing beside a waterhole; they had been for some time without water. Whether this is so or not, the sudden sight of the carpet of colour spread by these dancing, gay, abundant flowers, which are usually found near waterholes, could well have inspired it. Flowers of *Chorizema* are orange, pink, red and yellow. Often large, they are clustered in short-stemmed racemes, usually terminal. The broad spreading standard is circular or kidney-shaped, longer and much larger than the wings and keel. The fruit is a small soft inflated pod.

An unusual western genus of the pea family is *Brachysema,* with about fifteen species, all endemic to the southwest except for a few which extend across the desert into South Australia and the Northern Territory. Large flowers, in various shades of red, are usually carried solitary along the stems or occasionally in racemes. Unlike the typical pea-flower, the standard is small and inconspicuous, while the two lower petals which form the keel are large, close-fitting and prominent. The stamens are all free and the fruit is an inflated pod containing several seeds. Foliage is often interesting. Leaves are sometimes so reduced that the plant appears to be leafless and the flamboyant flowers seem to spring directly from flattened, ribbon-like stems, such as in *Brachysema aphyllum* (Plate 46), the ribbon pea. In some other species the leaves are large, and silvery underneath, and the buds are silvery also, giving the plant a two-toned effect, such as in *B. lanceolatum* (Plate 44), the dark pea bush. A curious member of the group is *B. daviesioides,* the upside-down peabush of inland sand plains, which has leafless, spiky, much-divided stems rising like a crown of thorns above a mat of large, orange-red flowers, clustered on the bare sand in crowded basal racemes.

Plate 42
HOLLY PEA—*Jacksonia floribunda*
This is a genus of leafless plants in which flattened stems, or cladodes, take over the function and sometimes the appearance of leaves. In many species flowers grow on the margins of the flattened stems; in the one pictured, however, they are carried in dense racemes, emerging sporadically from clusters of very hairy, greyish buds. Cladodes are broad and prickly, rather like a holly leaf in appearance.

Plate 43
HEART-LEAF FLAME PEA—*Chorizema cordatum*
A slender scrambling shrub with heart-shaped leaves, this plant is a native of the southwest and bears masses of brilliant orange, yellow and pink flowers in loose racemes in spring.

Plate 44
DARK PEA-BUSH—*Brachysema lanceolatum*
Also called the Swan River pea, a reference to the area in which it grows, this is an erect shrub which grows to two metres high in sandy or gravelly soil, especially along creeks. The dark green, lance-shaped leaves are silky-silvery beneath and the large, dark red, claw-shaped flowers, two to three centimetres long, are carried solitary or in small groups in the leaf axils.

42

43

44

Other large, wholly Australian genera of the pea family are *Daviesia,* commonly known as bitter peas, and *Oxylobium,* the shaggy peas, so-called because pods are often hairy. There are about thirty *Oxylobium* species, more than half of them endemic to the west. They range in habit from prostrate and wiry shrubs to small trees, such as *O. lanceolatum,* the native willow (Plate 45). Flowers of this genus are yellow or orange and stamens are free. Fruit is a small pointed pod and leaves are mostly opposite or in whorls of three. Foliage of many species is poisonous to stock. *Daviesia* is a genus of about seventy species of shrubs, more than fifty of which are confined to the southwest of Western Australia.

Flowers are small and yellow, blotched with reddish-orange; they are usually massed in axillary racemes and have inspired the alternative common name of eggs-and-bacon which they share with a number of other native pea-flowers. Stamens are free and the pods are flattened and characteristically triangular. In many species foliage has a strong bitter element, hence the common name, bitter peas, for the group as a whole. Leaves are alternate, sometimes broad and leathery, often reduced to sharp spines or inconspicuous scales. Two formidable western species are *D. reversifolia,* which has zigzagging stems with recurved, spiny leaves, and *D. pachyphylla* (the ouch bush) with its armoury of curiously inflated, silvery, sharp-pointed leaves.

Plate 45
NATIVE WILLOW—*Oxylobium lanceolatum*
The native willow is a tall shrub or small tree common along the banks of creeks and rivers in the southwest corner of the continent. It can grow to ten metres, but is mostly a shrub, two metres or less high. Deep yellow to orange flowers are borne in terminal racemes in spring and summer; the lanceolate leaves are up to eight centimetres long.

Plate 46
RIBBON PEA—*Brachysema aphyllum*
This is a prostrate shrub with flat, leafless stems and slender scarlet upturned flowers which can be up to five centimetres long. It occurs in heath country of the northern sand plains.

Family RUTACEAE

The Boronias

This is a highly aromatic family; it includes the citrus fruits—lemon, lime, cumquat, orange and grapefruit—the curry plant of Ceylon and the rue of medieval times—symbol of repentance and Shakespeare's 'herb of grace'—from which the family name derives. Despite this history in the Old World, however, more than half of the family Rutaceae belong to warm temperate parts of the southern hemisphere, and of these the majority are indigenous to Australia—most of them endemic.

They are also abundant in South Africa, where most of the remaining southern species are to be found. In the main these southern members of the Rutaceae belong to the tribe Boronieae, though Australia does have its own native citrus (*Microcitrus*), one species of which grows in the Kimberley district of the northwest and bears a small orange-like fruit.

All members of the Rutaceae, from tangerine to boronia, from rue to curry to the tall rainforest trees of the east coast, such as Australian teak (*Flindersia australis*) and Queensland maple (*F. brayleyana*), have one easily recognisable factor in common—highly aromatic foliage and the presence of oil glands which can be seen as tiny translucent dots when the leaves are held up to the light. Another clue to identity is the superior lobed ovary (seedbox) which is elevated on a disc rather like a tiny crown on a cushion.

Flowers of Rutaceae mostly have four or five sepals (calyx segments) and an equal number of petals. This is often a guide to identification of genus. *Boronia,* for example, has four sepals and four petals; *Eriostemon* has five. Leaves may be alternate or opposite—in *Boronia* they are opposite, in *Eriostemon,* alternate. Flowers of the Rutaceae are of many colours, often pink but also white, yellow, red, brown and, rarely, green or blue. They are frequently sweetly scented. Sepals are often united at the base to form a cup-like calyx. The four or five petals are mostly spreading and star-like but in some *Boronia* species they are arranged in a bell-like manner. Stamens are either equal in number to the petals, or double in number; they are rarely more numerous. In the western genus *Diplolaena* many small flowers with long bright stamens are crowded into heads surrounded by petal-like bracts, so that the whole resembles a many-stamened single flower, and in *Geleznowia,* another western genus, what appears to be a single flower is

Plate 47
WINGED BORONIA—*Boronia alata*
This boronia has pinnate leaves, narrowly winged along the common stalk; foliage is highly aromatic and the lavender-pink flowers, with their four pointed petals, are carried in umbels from mid-spring to mid-summer. A common shrub throughout the southwest, it grows from one to three metres in height.

Plate 48
BROWN BORONIA—*Boronia megastigma*
Also known as the scented boronia, these highly perfumed flowers are widely cultivated in areas far distant from the limited area of the southwest to which they were confined in nature; so much so, in fact, that it is often called 'Melbourne boronia' because it is grown so extensively in and around that city. A small slender shrub, usually no more than a metre high, it has small narrow leaves and cup-shaped brown and yellow flowers. Its natural habitat is the sandy swamps of the southwest, and it flowers in early spring.

usually a cluster of two or three, surrounded by colourful yellow or orange-brown bracts (Plate 49). Largest Australian genus in the Rutaceae is *Boronia,* with about sixty or seventy species. None occur outside this continent, and about half the species are confined to Western Australia. Leaves are opposite, simple or divided. Foliage is highly aromatic. More even than the eucalypts, the pungent odour of crushed *Boronia* foliage is the epitome of the Australian bush. Strong, at times even rank, it is the almost inevitable accompaniment of a walk through the bush.

Many *Boronia* species bear highly perfumed flowers, notably the Western Australian brown boronia, *B. megastigma* (Plate 48) which occurs in a limited area in the southwest and has sweetly scented, cup-shaped flowers, rich chocolate brown outside and lemon-gold within. Most *Boronia* flowers are pink but quite a few western species are blue, brown or yellow. Floral parts are in fours— four sepals, four petals, eight stamens. The deeply lobed ovary has four segments. The calyx is small, and forms a plate-like support for the flowers. Petals are free, often widespread in starry fashion but sometimes incurved at the tips in a cup shape.

The genus *Eriostemon* has close affinities with *Boronia,* but species can easily be distinguished by the fact that *Eriostemon* have five petals, ten stamens and a five-lobed calyx. Leaves are always alternate, simple and entire. Flowers, usually some shade of pink, sometimes lavender or almost white, are mostly open and star-like, borne solitary in leaf axils or at the ends of branches. With the exception of one species, which extends to New Caledonia, *Eriostemon* is also a wholly Australian genus. There are about thirty species, about half of them indigenous to the west, where they are commonly known as pepper-and-salt plants. Most western species are pink or mauve, but *E. nodiflorus,* found in wet sandy areas of the southwest, is sometimes bright blue.

There are only six *Diplolaena* species and all are confined to Western Australia. Numerous long-stamened, brightly coloured yellow, orange or red flowers are crowded into pendant heads and enclosed by multiple rows of greenish, petal-like bracts. *D. angustifolia,* the Yanchep rose, has crimson to pale orange stamens up to three centimetres long, in heads about as wide. *D. dampieri,* the southern rose, has a slightly smaller flowerhead and large leaves, softly furry underneath. It grows on the sand dunes of the southwest and was one of the few Australian native plants collected by Dampier in 1699.

Plate 49
A GELEZNOWIA—*Geleznowia verrucosa*
 A small shrub to thirty centimetres high, this colourful plant owes its appeal to bright yellow, persistent bracts which enclose and conceal the cluster of small flowers. It grows in sandy heathlands north of Perth.

Family EUPHORBIACEAE
The Spurges

This is an immense family, widespread throughout the world, with around 300 genera and nearly 8,000 species. Members are trees, shrubs and herbs, usually with an acrid, milky juice. Some are poisonous, but many have been used medicinally as emetics, purgatives, and so on. From this family come rubber and tung oil, castor oil and tapioca, starches and dyes. It also includes many lovely ornamentals, such as poinsettia and crown-of-thorns (*Euphorbia* spp.). Flowers of the family have four to six sepals, and petals, when present, also number four to six. Often, however, they are absent or insignificant, their decorative role assumed by other parts of the plant—modified leaves, or highly coloured bracts.

In Australia the family is mainly represented in the rainforests of the east, but about twenty-six genera and some hundred-odd species occur in the west, including the majority of Australia's thirty or so indigenous *Euphorbia* species. The genus *Ricinocarpus,* however, is with the exception of one species in New Caledonia, wholly confined to Australia, with the majority of its species in temperate areas of the west.

Family POLYGALACEAE
The Milkworts

The milkworts are an almost cosmopolitan family of herbs, shrubs or small trees. Flowers bear a superficial resemblance to the pea-flowers of the Fabaceae (formerly Papilionaceae) but the 'butterfly' wings are not petals at all but large, wing-like, colourful sepals, while the innermost petals are more or less united to form a keel. The family includes some ornamentals, such as *Polygala myrtifolia,* the sweetpea bush from South Africa, and members of this genus have long been viewed with favour in Europe because, it was said, they helped promote the flow of milk in domestic animals—hence the common name, milkworts, for the family as a whole. The family is also valuable as a source of a number of useful drugs.

Australia has several *Polygala* species, mainly across the tropical north, but the major Australian genus is the wholly endemic *Comesperma,* with about twenty-four species of shrubs and twining plants, more than half of which are confined to the southwest corner of the continent.

Plate 50
BRIDAL BUSH—*Ricinocarpus glaucus*
This small attractive shrub occurs in the southwest generally and is common in the karri forests. There are about fifteen endemic Australian species of *Ricinocarpus,* ten of which can be found in the west. Known as the wedding bushes, they are small erect shrubs with alternate, entire and often narrow leaves. Flowers are unisexual and grow in terminal clusters. Both male and female occur on the same plant, and can be distinguished from one another by the presence of stamens in the male flower and a superior ovary in the female. Fruit is a rough, bristly, globular capsule which when ripe splits open, explosively scattering three mottled, shiny, oily seeds.

Plate 51
MILKWORT—*Comesperma virgatum*
A graceful, erect shrub which grows to about a metre in height, this plant is common in swampy or low-lying sandy situations of the southwest. It carries dense racemes of lilac to purple pea-like flowers on long slender stems throughout spring and summer.

50

51

Family STERCULIACEAE

The Kurrajongs

A widely dispersed family, occurring mainly in tropical regions and particularly abundant in Australia and South Africa, the Sterculiaceae is a family of shrubs, herbs and trees, closely related to the Malvaceae (Hibiscus family). There are some fifty genera (about half of them indigenous to Australia) and over 1,200 species. Cocoa and chocolate are extracted from the seeds of a Central American species and cola from a native of west Africa. Some species yield valuable gums, others are a source of useful cabinet timbers.

Flowers may be either bisexual or unisexual and sometimes all types—male, female and bisexual flowers—are borne on the same plant. Floral parts are in fives; five sepals, usually large, petal-like and fused into a colourful bell-shaped calyx, five petals, always very small and sometimes absent altogether, and five to fifteen stamens.

The best known Australian genera are *Brachychiton, Lasiopetalum* and *Thomasia,* all of which are entirely confined to this continent and well represented in the west. *Brachychiton,* a genus of about twelve species, includes tall rainforest trees of the east coast such as the Illawarra flame tree (*Brachychiton acerifolium*). Western species are mainly from the tropical north, such as the broadleafed bottle tree, *B. australe,* but include the common kurrajong, *B. gregorii,* of the drier inland areas. There are about thirty *Lasiopetalum* species, all confined to Australia and the majority of them endemic to the west. They are commonly called velvet bushes because of the soft velvety hairs, often rusty red in colour, which in many species cover branches, foliage and flowers. *Thomasia*

species are the so-called paper flowers; petals are absent or minute and the dilated, colourful sepals are dry and paper-thin. There are about twenty-eight species, all confined to the southwest of Western Australia except one, which extends into South Australia and Victoria.

Family DILLENIACEAE

The Guinea-flowers

The Dilleniaceae is closely allied to the buttercup family, Ranunculaceae. The largest genus, *Hibbertia,* with about 120 species, is almost exclusively Australian. About sixty species are endemic in the southwest of Western Australia, two are known from the Kimberleys and one from the Hamersley Range. Flowers of Dilleniaceae have five persistent sepals, five petals and numerous stamens. *Hibbertia* species are shrubs, undershrubs and twiners; flowers are almost always yellow, with soft, spreading petals.

Plate 52
LITTLE PAPER FLOWER—*Thomasia pauciflora*
This is a plant of the karri forests of the southwest, a shrub which grows from one to two metres high and bears racemes of mauve to purple flowers in mid-winter and spring.

Plate 53
CUTLEAF HIBBERTIA—*Hibbertia cuneiformis*
Hibbertia species, the golden guinea flowers, are a conspicuous feature of the southern heathlands of Western Australia. The one pictured is common in the karri forests and is one of the tallest, a shrub three or four metres high, with large smooth shining leaves, wedge-shaped and lightly toothed, and yellow flowers two to three centimetres across. It blooms from early spring to late summer.

52

53

Family THYMELAEACEAE

The Daphne family

This is a cosmopolitan family, most abundant in Africa and Australia but with representatives even in Arctic regions. It includes the sweetly scented daphne of English gardens, which was introduced into Britain from Japan in the eighteenth century. Many species have tough fibres, sometimes used in the manufacture of quality writing paper, especially in Japan. Australian Aboriginals used the bark from native species (notably the banjine of Western Australia) for making cords. Members are mostly shrubs or trees, rarely herbs, with alternate or opposite, simple and entire leaves. Flowers are tubular or bell-shaped, with four spreading lobes; they consist of a seemingly single whorl of joined sepals—petals are absent or scale-like.

Two genera occur in Western Australia, the largest being the mainly Australian genus *Pimelea*, with about eighty species endemic to this continent, about half of them confined to the west. The other genus present is *Wikstroemia*, in the tropical north of the State. *Pimelea* are shrubs or undershrubs with small tubular flowers consisting of four petaloid sepals; petals are absent. With few exceptions, the flowers are massed in terminal heads surrounded by petal-like bracts. When these bracts do not obscure the true flowers, as in the species pictured (Plates 54 and 55), the inflorescence is pincushion-like, and these species are commonly known as riceflowers, a reference to the granular appearance of the dense, often white, flowerheads. Where the bracts are longer and obscure the flowerheads, the involucre is drooping and bell-like, such as in the dramatic qualup bell (*P. physodes*) which has colourful bracts, in tones of greenish yellow and purple-red and up to five centimetres long, surrounding and obscuring a cluster of several true flowers. Some *Pimelea* species, like their cousin the daphne, have sweetly scented flowers; one such is the western *P. suaveolens,* the silky yellow banjine of the jarrah forests, which has large 'riceflower' heads up to four centimetres across. Some of the taller kinds, such as *P. clavata,* the 'banjine' of the Aboriginals, can provide long strips of very tough bark, and some are called 'bootlace bushes' for this reason.

Plate 54
COASTAL BANJINE—*Pimelea ferruginea*
This pink-flowered *Pimelea* is a bushy shrub which grows up to a metre in height in sandy and granite country of the southwest. It blooms from early spring to late summer.

Plate 55
ROSE BANJINE—*Pimelea rosea* (white form)
Pimelea rosea, as its name implies, is typically a pink-flowered shrub, and is common on the coastal plain from Perth to Albany. However, in the jarrah forests, it is always white-flowered, and this is the form pictured here. A shrub which grows to one metre in height, it has soft, linear leaves and flowerheads up to three centimetres across, borne from early spring to mid-summer.

54

55

Family MYRTACEAE

The Myrtles

The Myrtaceae is the largest family of flowering plants in the flora of Australia. It includes the ever-present gumtrees (*Eucalyptus* spp.) so dominant in the Australian landscape—only in the rainforests and the near-desert areas of the arid interior are they absent or overshadowed by a greater abundance of other genera. The bottlebrush flowers of *Callistemon* and *Melaleuca* belong to the Myrtaceae; so do the tea-trees (*Leptospermum* spp.) and the unique mountain bells of the Stirling Range (*Darwinia* spp.), the round-petalled glassy-pink waxflowers (*Chamelaucium* spp.), the softly-fringed featherflowers (*Verticordia* spp.) and many, many others. In all, there are more than fifty Australian genera and well over 1,000 species, all woody but ranging in size from prostrate shrubs to giant trees, such as the karri (*Eucalyptus diversicolor*) of southwest Western Australia, which grows to a height of almost 100 metres.

The family is represented in warmer parts of both hemispheres, but there is a remarkable development of types peculiar to Australia and indeed it has been suggested that the Myrtaceae may have originated here and migrated elsewhere before the land links with the rest of the world were severed. Although there is little definite evidence to support this, it is a fascinating thought. If true, some of those emigrant myrtles now return from abroad in the form of cloves, dried flowerbuds of an East Indian *Eugenia*—the spices of the Orient which have played a major part in human intercourse since earliest times.

A striking feature of many members of the Myrtaceae is the role of the stamens in the attractiveness of the flowers, even when petals are present and relatively large. Stamens are mostly long and numerous; petals are frequently small and sometimes absent. In some groups of *Eucalyptus,* the petals are fused in bud to form the operculum or cap (the generic name, from the Greek *eu,* well; *kalyptos,* covered, refers to this cap over the bud). In other groups the operculum consists of fused sepals, or there may be an outer cap of sepals and an inner one of petals. Whichever the case, this cap is forced off when the flower opens; petals and sepals are shed altogether and the crowded, often colourful stamens are the most conspicuous feature of the gum blossom. In the bottlebrush flowers of *Callistemon* and *Calothamnus,* once again the stamens play the prominent part. Petals are tiny, pale-coloured or greenish, sometimes deciduous and always inconspicuous—the flowerheads are showy because of the numerous long stamens.

The family can be divided into two distinct sections: the Myrtoideae, with berry-like fruit, such as the Australian eugenias and lillypillies, and the Leptospermoideae, the fruit of which is a dry, often woody capsule—the familiar gumnut is a typical example. The Myrtoideae is mainly tropical in distribution. South America is the major centre of

Plate 56

MOTTLECAH—*Eucalyptus macrocarpa*
The spectacular gold-tipped crimson flowers of the mottlecah are ten to fifteen centimetres across, the largest of all the eucalypts. They are stalkless and carried singly in the axis of decorative, silvery-grey, stem-clasping leaves. This species is one that retains juvenile-type foliage in maturity; leaves are opposite and arranged more or less in fours along mealy branches. The mottlecah is a mallee-type eucalypt of the sand heaths north and east of Perth, a straggling, shrubby tree often little more than a metre high.

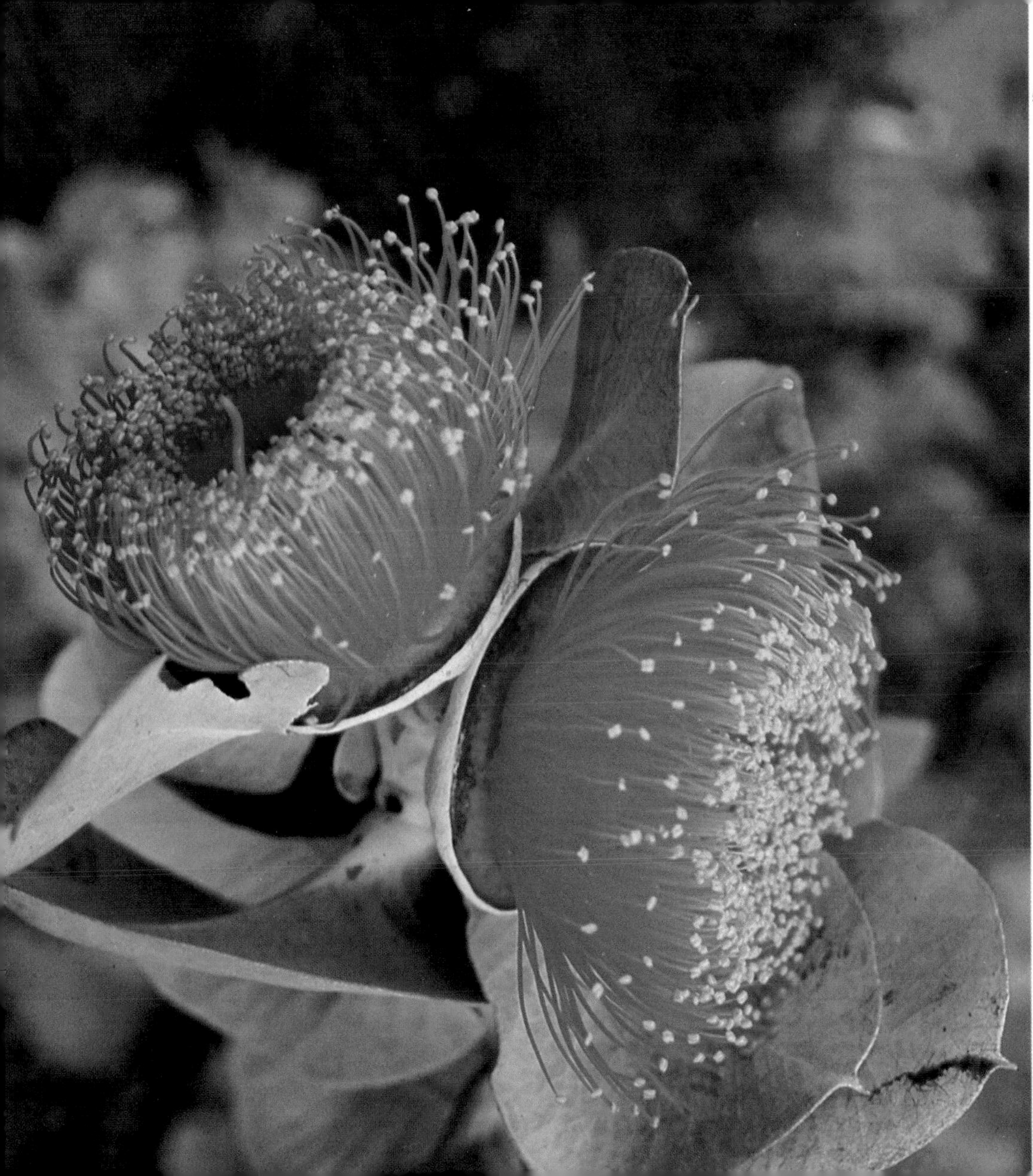

development (the allspice of commerce is the dried, unripe berry of a Central American species). In Western Australia it is represented by several *Eugenia* species in the tropical north but, in the main, Australian genera of this subfamily are to be found in the warm moist rainforests of the east coast.

The vast majority of Australian members belong to the subfamily Leptospermoideae which is almost exclusively Australian—there are only minor extensions eastwards to New Zealand and New Caledonia, and northwards to Indonesia, the Philippines and Malaysia. Members are typically the heat-resisting plants of dry places, and are characterised by many adaptations to conserve moisture. Fruit is a dry capsule. Leaves are tough, with thick cuticles, often hairy, reduced or crowded; many hang vertically, turned sideways to the sun's rays. Oil glands are usually present.

The largest Australian genus is *Eucalyptus,* with at least 400 species. Eucalypts predominate in more than nine-tenths of Australia's total forest area. They range over thousands of square kilometres of country, from rich coastal plains and hot tropical areas to the dry interior. The genus is almost exclusively Australian. Only half a dozen species occur naturally outside this country and these are confined to New Guinea and nearby islands to the north. None occur in New Zealand.

There are about 160 *Eucalyptus* species in Western Australia, ranging from desert mallees less than a metre high to the giant hardwoods in the forests of the southwest. Eucalypts are commonly grouped according to bark, timber, or other convenient features. Many species, chiefly those with smooth bark, are called gums—rather a misnomer since no true gum is obtained from any eucalypt. The sticky dark red exudation seen in many is kino, a resinous

material containing tannin. It is particularly abundant in some rough-barked eucalypts which are commonly known as bloodwoods for that reason. *Eucalyptus dichromophloia,* the variable-barked bloodwood, grows in the brilliant dry sunshine of northwest inland areas. A prolific honey-producer, it flowers in autumn, weighed down with blossoms so copiously filled with nectar that the honey drips on the ground. The most striking example of the smooth-barked gums is probably *Eucalyptus papuana,* the ghost gum. This is the typical eucalypt of the dry northern interior. A short-boled tree with spreading branches, it grows up to about twenty metres in height. The stark white moulded trunk and wide-flung boughs, ghostly against its natural background of brilliant blue sky and harsh red landscape, have inspired the common name.

Mallee is the term applied to many scrubby eucalypts tending to develop numerous slender stems rather than one main shaft. These spring from a much-enlarged woody underground rootstock (lignotuber) which is protected from

Plate 57
CORAL GUM—*Eucalyptus torquata*
The coral gum is a small rough-barked tree, three to five metres tall, which grows in the low rainfall country around Kalgoorlie and Norseman. The main attraction lies in the coral-pink, oddly shaped buds which are two to three centimetres long.

Plate 58
TALLERACK—*Eucalyptus tetragona*
Buds are a striking feature of this mallee also; pale green, they are covered with a soft down of bluish grey, and the leaves and four-winged stems as well. Flowers are creamy white. It is found on the southern sand heaths from around Albany to Esperance.

58

57

bushfires and extremes of heat and cold and also acts as a storehouse of food and nourishment during dry periods. This mallee form of growth is the tree's answer to harsh conditions; many eucalypts, in adversity, have the potential to maintain themselves as mallees, though normally single-trunked, and the reverse is also true—often true mallees, when grown under ideal conditions are capable of developing as a single trunk. Many mallees are noted for the size and brilliance of their flowers, which often seem to be in inverse proportion to the insignificance of the straggling bushes that bear them. The mottlecah (*Eucalyptus macrocarpa*, Plate 56) is often a low bedraggled shrub little more than a metre high (though it can grow as a white-barked tree up to five metres or so). Its spectacular crimson and gold flowers, ten to fifteen centimetres across, are the largest of the genus, indeed, the largest of any Australian Myrtaceae.

At the opposite extreme are the shaft-like timber trees of the high rainfall country of the southwest; the jarrah, *Eucalyptus marginata,* prized for its hard, dark red, durable timber, and the karri, *E. diversicolor,* one of the world's tallest hardwoods, which grows to ninety metres—a height exceeded only marginally by *E. regnans,* the mighty mountain ash of southeastern Australia. Both have relatively small flowers, often inconspicuous among the foliage.

In most *Eucalyptus* species, leaves of young saplings are vastly different to those of the mature tree. Juvenile leaves, often bluish-grey in colour, quite often broad and stalkless, are always more or less opposite. In certain species (*E. macrocarpa* is one) this juvenile foliage is maintained throughout the life of the tree, but in the majority of species it is progressively discarded and replaced with mature

leaves which are typically sickle-shaped and mostly alternate. They are tough, usually hang vertically, and have a pronounced marginal vein. If the tree is damaged by bushfire or cutting, the sucker growth reverts to the juvenile foliage and both types are sometimes seen on the same tree.

Economically, the eucalypts are of great importance. They include many of the world's best hardwoods and some are used in the manufacture of pulp, paper and hardboard. Many are important honey trees, valued as a source of both nectar and pollen. Leaves of some species yield valuable essential oils, and the kino (gum) has some pharmaceutical use as an astringent. Scores of very lovely eucalypts are extensively cultivated both in Australia and abroad; they are prized for their hardiness as well as their ornamental appeal.

A number of genera in the Myrtaceae are exclusively Western Australian. The genus *Chamaelaucium* is in this group, all the fifteen-odd species being endemic to the southwest corner of the State. It is one of about a dozen allied genera which are either entirely confined to the west or have their greatest development and almost certainly had their origin there; they are classified by some botanists in a separate group, the Chamaelaucieae.

Commonly called waxflowers, *Chamaelaucium* species have five-petalled flowers, which are

Plate 59
GERALDTON WAXFLOWER—
Chamaelaucium uncinatum
As the common name implies, this plant, with its dainty, waxen, five-petalled flowers of delicate pink, grows naturally on the coastal sand plains near Geraldton. A bushy shrub which grows from one to five metres in height, it is now commonly cultivated in gardens.

always stiff and waxy and coloured pink, white or red. Stamens are ten in number and leaves are always small and narrow. Best known member of the genus is the Geraldton waxflower, *C. uncinatum* (Plate 59). This is the tallest of the species and grows from one to five metres in height. Largest-flowered is the Esperance waxflower, *C. megalopetalum*, from the southern extreme of this botanically rich southwest province. A much lower plant, rarely more than a metre high, its flowers are one to two centimetres across, white at first and later turning red.

The genus *Calothamnus* (Plate 60) is also entirely restricted to Western Australia. There are about twenty-four species, all in the south; most are richly coloured, crimson and other shades of red and pink. Flowers consist of long, conspicuous stamens, united into flattened bundles for portion of their length, free and feathery at the top, and enclosed by five small petals and five small calyx lobes. They are usually arranged on the branch in a one-sided manner, sometimes partly embedded, and are commonly called one-sided bottlebrushes or clawflowers for this reason. One of the showiest is *C. homalophyllus*, the Murchison clawflower, which grows to two metres tall on sandy or rocky ground from Geraldton to the Murchison River; the bundles of deep red stamens, three to four centimetres long, are borne in spring. *C. quadrifidus*, known as the one-sided bottlebrush, has rich crimson stamens and dark green, pine-like foliage. The commonest and most widespread of the genus, its range extends from the Murchison River to beyond Esperance on the south coast, and its blooms are carried from mid-summer to mid-winter. The species pictured, *C. chrysantherus*, extends further north than any other and across the red sand plains of the inland. A small shrub less

than a metre high, it flowers throughout winter and early spring.

Another wholly western genus is *Beaufortia*, with sixteen species. These consist of shrubs with papery bark and bottlebrush-type flowers, the stamens united in flattened bundles with the upper ends free, as in *Calothamnus*, but carried in terminal, fluffy heads. *Beaufortia sparsa*, the swamp bottlebrush of the Albany coast, is one of the most striking; it flowers from mid-summer to late autumn, bearing vermillion-red flowerheads up to six centimetres or more across.

There are about twelve species in the genus *Hypocalymma*, all endemic to the southwest of Western Australia. Commonly called myrtles, they have flowers with five spreading petals, usually white, pink or yellow, and numerous long, loose stamens which give the flower a fluffy appearance though they do not outrival the petals, as in many of the Myrtaceae. Best known is the Swan River myrtle, *H. robustum*, a common small shrub of the Darling Range and adjacent coastal plains. It grows to a height of about a metre and has sweetly scented pink flowers, about one centimetre across, which are carried in small axillary clusters in late winter and spring.

Plate 60
A CLAWFLOWER—*Calothamnus chrysantherus*
The most conspicuous part of this flower is the long, brightly coloured stamens, which are united into flattened bundles on the lower portion, and free and feathery at the tip. It is a small shrub, less than a metre in height, found on the red sand plains north and east of Perth. Flowers are borne in winter and early spring.

in colour, which persists after the petals wither to form the shining 'copper cups' from which the common name derives. Stamens are twenty in number, and in some species are forked.

The summer coppercup, *P. filifolius* (Plate 63), is the largest-flowered species, with blossoms of intense pink, up to two centimetres across. A slender shrub which grows to about a metre in height, it occurs on the sand heaths north of Perth and flowers throughout the summer months. *P. penuncularis,* the common coppercup, is spring-flowering, with glowing orange blooms about one centimetre in diameter; a spreading shrub about fifty centimetres tall, it has a wider distribution on the sand plains north and east of Perth. The coastal coppercup, *P. limacis,* extends further north again to Shark Bay and Exmouth Gulf. This was the first species collected, by the French botanist Leschenault, on the Baudin expedition which called at Shark Bay in 1801. It is far less vividly coloured than the other species, flowers being pale pink or creamy.

Darwinia is a genus of about thirty-five species, mostly confined to Western Australia but with some representatives in South Australia and eastern mainland States. None occurs in Tasmania. It also differs from the majority of the Myrtaceae in that stamens are not the main floral attraction, but are small and inconspicuous; in *Darwinia* it is the bracts around the flowers, and often the pistils, that are showy. The style, often bearded, extends well beyond the floral tube, and flowers are sometimes clustered into close heads at the ends of branches, giving the inflorescence a pincushion appearance, such as in *D. vestita,* the pink and white pom-pom darwinia, which grows on the sand heaths from Albany to Esperance, and the green-flowered *D. virescens* of the Murchison River. In a very limited area, the Stirling Range in the south of

74

Western Australia, there are several *Darwinia* species in which the flowerheads are completely enclosed by enormous colourful bracts which form pendulous tulip-like flowerheads up to five centimetres long. These are the mountain bells and each main peak in the range has its own distinctive species.

Plate 63
SUMMER COPPERCUP—*Pileanthus filifolius*
The summer coppercup is a shrub with small, rounded, pointed leaves which grows to a metre high in the sandy heath country between Perth and Geraldton. It is the largest-flowered of the genus. The common name, coppercups, is an allusion to the coppery-coloured, ten-lobed calyx which persists after the flowers wither, as can be seen in this photograph.

Plate 64
FIERY BOTTLEBRUSH—*Callistemon phoeniceus*
This is one of only two *Callistemon* species found in the west. Both are endemic. It is a tall shrub, up to three or four metres high, with a range from Carnarvon in the north to Norseman in the east, and almost to the south coast. The fiery flowerheads, ten to fifteen centimetres long, are one of the most brilliantly coloured of all Australia's bottlebrushes, and are commonly cultivated in gardens.

Plate 65
LEMON-SCENTED MYRTLE—*Darwinia citriodora*
Several *Darwinia* species contain a highly perfumed, lemon-scented volatile oil and, as the common name implies, this is one. A bushy shrub which grows to about two metres tall in the sandy loams of the southwest, it carries its striking scarlet and green flowers from mid-winter to summer.

63

64

65

Callistemon is a wholly Australian genus of about twenty species of shrubs and small trees in the family Myrtaceae, two of which are endemic to the west. Numerous individual flowers are carried in dense, cylindrical, 'bottlebrush' spikes at the tips of branches. The shoot continues to grow from the apex, and downy new foliage soon protrudes beyond the flower spike—a characteristic also of many bottlebrush-flowered melaleucas. The following season a new flower spike forms at the growing tip, and the woody cup-like fruit of the earlier flowers remains clustered in solid masses lower down the branch. These capsules remain on the tree indefinitely—in many cases they do not open and release seed unless the branch or plant is damaged—and the age of the specimen can usually be determined by counting the successive clusters. Flowers of the two western *Callistemon* species are vivid crimson (though eastern species include white, creamy-yellow, pink, mauve and even pale green flowers). There are five very inconspicuous petals and numerous colourful, much longer, free stamens, which are the main attraction of the inflorescence (the generic name means 'beautiful stamen', from the Greek *kallos*, beauty, and *stemon,* stamen). Leaves are stiff, long, narrow and crowded. Both the western species are found on the margins of swamps and watercourses; *C. speciosus,* the Albany bottlebrush, is common around that area, and *C. phoeniceus* (Plate 64) extends further, to the Gascoyne River and Carnarvon in the north, and Norseman in the east.

The closely related genus *Melaleuca* has more than 150 species, all Australian and all confined to this continent except one, which extends to the East Indies. This is *M. leucadendron,* the cajeput tree, from which comes the cajeput oil of commerce. It is widespread across the tropical north, and reaches a height of about twenty metres. The genus reaches its greatest development in Western Australia, where there are about 100 species, most of them endemic. As with *Callistemon,* there are five small petals, but in *Melaleuca* the prominent colourful stamens are not free but are united at the base into five bundles which are placed opposite the five petals. Flowers may be arranged in bottlebrush spikes, like those of *Callistemon,* or in rounded heads or small clusters along the stems and at the ends of branches. Colours range from white, through cream, yellow and various shades of pink, mauve and purple to brilliant reds. Leaves are variable, sometimes opposite and sometimes alternate, ranging from tiny and crowded to large and broad. A characteristic of most species of *Melaleuca* is the spongy, papery bark, which can be stripped off in layers—many are commonly called paperbarks for this reason. The generic name, from the Greek, *mel,* black, and *leuca,* white, aptly describes them because the outer bark of the trunk is often black, charred by bushfires, while the inner layers and bark on the branches is usually white.

Kunzeas belong to the myrtle family. There are about twenty-five species, all confined to Australia and about half of them endemic to the west. Flowers have five petals, but these are always small and the numerous stamens are always considerably longer; stamens are free, as in *Callistemon.* Kunzeas are mostly heath-like shrubs; flowers may be white,

Plate 66
GRACEFUL HONEY-MYRTLE—*Melaleuca radula*
One of the 'bottlebrush' type melaleucas, this is a shrub, one to two metres tall, with stiff little branches that bend with the weight of the numerous flowerheads, giving the plant a most graceful appearance. Leaves are opposite, and the gold-tipped, lilac flowerheads are carried in opposite pairs.

pink, mauve, red or yellow, and leaves are mostly small, narrow and alternate. Fruit is a capsule; usually three-celled, it opens at the top and is crowned by persistent sepals.

There are about forty *Calytrix* species, starry flowers of the Myrtaceae commonly called fringe myrtles. Mostly small shrubs, they are all confined to Australia, the majority of them to the west, though one or two species occur in every State. Flowers have five star-like petals, alternating with five sepals, which are joined together at the base to form a shallow cup, tapering off at each lobe into a long fine, hairlike point. Stamens are numerous. Fruit is a small nut, surmounted by the persistent calyx which remains after the petals drop, enlarging and changing colour, often in quite spectacular fashion, as the fruit matures.

Eremaea is a genus of about ten small shrubs, all endemic to the southwest and mostly found in the northern parts of that area. The pom-pom flowers of crowded stamens are sometimes solitary, sometimes grouped in globular heads which resemble those of *Kunzea* and *Melaleuca*. Mostly they are bright orange but in some species are purple, violet or pink. They differ from the above genera mainly in the botanical structure of the anthers. Seeds are angular, with fringed margins.

Family UMBELLIFERAE

The Carrot family

This family includes many food plants—carrots, parsnips, celery and culinary herbs and spices such as parsley, caraway, aniseed and dill. Fennel and poison hemlock are also members. It is most prominent in the northern hemisphere, but is represented in most other parts of the world.

Western Australian members include *Actinotus,* the flannel flowers, an exclusively Australian genus with main centres of development in the southwest of Western Australia and coastal New South Wales. Other genera in the west are *Eryngium* (blue devils), *Trachymene* (*T. caerulea* is the dainty blue lace flower of coastal limestone country around Perth) and *Xanthosia,* which includes the spectacular four-rayed southern cross (Plate 68).

Flowers of this family are very small and arranged in umbels, radiating like the ribs of an umbrella from the apex of a common stem. Sometimes a number of these simple umbels are in turn arranged in a larger, complex umbel, such as in *Xanthosia rotundifolia* (pictured) and sometimes the umbels are surrounded by an involucre of petal-like bracts, as in *Actinotus,* the daisy-like flannel flowers.

Plate 67
RUSTY EREMAEA—*Eremaea acutifolia*
The bright flowers of *Eremaea acutifolia* are carried solitary at the ends of short branches. One of several orange-flowered eremaeas, it is a small shrub which grows to about fifty centimetres on the sand heaths near Geraldton.

Plate 68
SOUTHERN CROSS—*Xanthosia rotundifolia*
This unusual inflorescence is known botanically as a four-rayed compound umbel. It consists of clusters of tiny individual flowers, carried on slender stalks radiating from the apex of a common stem. The four equal arms are arranged on one plane, like a cross, and each cluster is sheathed with conspicuous, petal-like bracts. *Xanthosia rotundifolia* is a perennial herb which grows to about fifty centimetres tall. The large toothed leaves are oval to wedge-shaped.

67

68

Family EPACRIDACEAE

The Australian Heaths

The Epacridaceae is a family of heath-like shrubs and a few small trees, mainly confined to Australia and closely allied to the true heath family of the Old World (Ericaceae). The family name, from the genus *Epacris,* means 'on a hilltop' (Greek *epi,* upon; *akris,* hill-top) and refers to the fact that these plants are often found on stony ridges. They show special adaptation to dry conditions (though some species are found in swamps). Leaves are mostly stiff, small and crowded, often sharp-pointed or thickened at the tip. An unusual feature is the apparently parallel venation, similar to that of a blade of grass—actually veins are not parallel in the true sense but diverge from the same point at the base of the leaf.

Flowers are regular and floral parts are in fives. Petals are always united into a tube, with five free lobes. This floral tube is usually long, sometimes swollen in the middle so that the flower is cup-like rather than bell-shaped or tubular. Occasionally it is so short as to be little more than a ring. The lobes at the tip of the corolla may be short or they may be spreading and star-like. The five stamens are in most cases attached to the petals. Fruit is usually five-celled and is either a capsule or a berry-like, succulent drupe.

The largest Australian genus is *Leucopogon,* with about 150 endemic species, over 100 of which are confined to the southwest of Western Australia. These are the beard heaths, so-called because the inside surface of the petal-lobes is densely clothed with white hairs. *Andersonia* is a purely Western genus of twenty-two species of small shrubs with stem-clasping, sharply pointed leaves. Largest is *A. axilliflora,* which grows to two metres and is confined to the eastern peaks of the Stirling Range. The young leaves at the tips of the erect stems are interesting; triangular and up to six centimetres long, they are creamy-white, sometimes green-tipped, and enclose the small creamy flowers. Other *Andersonia* species have pink, blue or red flowers.

Other epacrid genera found in the west are *Sphenotoma,* with six endemic species, and *Astroloma,* with about twenty species, all but a few of which are confined to the southwest. *Sphenotoma* are the paper-heaths, with showy white flowers which become papery when old; they are commonly found in bogs and stony places. *Astroloma* are the native cranberries; the attractive tubular flowers are in various shades of pink, orange, red, as well as white or creamy, and fruit is a succulent, edible drupe.

Plate 69
TASSEL FLOWER—*Leucopogon verticillatus*
A shrub up to four metres tall, the tassel flower is the largest of Western Australia's 100-odd *Leucopogon* species. The unusually large, broad leaves, up to fifteen centimetres long, are attractively coloured when young, and the tassels of flowers are sweetly scented. It blooms in spring.

Plate 70
FOXTAIL HEATH—*Andersonia caerulea*
The foxtail is a small dense shrub (to fifty centimetres) which carries its spikes of pink and blue flowers practically all the year round, but mainly in winter. Also known as the blue swamp heath, it is found on sand and gravel, in swampy situations in the southwest.

69

70

Family VERBENACEAE

The Verbena family

The Verbenaceae is a large family of herbs, shrubs and trees, chiefly tropical and subtropical. Foliage is usually odorous, sometimes pleasantly spicy, and stems and twigs are often squared. Members range from the little verbenas of garden borders to the teak of commerce, *Tectona grandis*, one of the world's most valuable timber trees. Common lantana, the rogue garden escapee that has invaded the the bushland of eastern Australia, also belongs to this family, as does the sweetly-scented white mangrove, *Avicennia marina*, of tidal mudflats around the Australian coast.

Western Australian representatives, however, are mainly in a group of their own, vastly different from the teak of tropical forests and the mangroves of the muddy estuaries. There is a remarkable development of the Verbenaceae in the State, with a number of mostly endemic genera of densely felted, woolly, or in other ways drought-resistant shrubs of the dry country, many of which are commonly called lambstails, a reference to the close-packed, woolly spikes in which the tiny flowers are concealed.

In this 'lambstail' group, which includes *Dicrastyles, Lachnostachys, Newcastlia* and *Physopsis*, stems and leaves are covered in dense, much-brnched hairs, and the flowers, which are carried in spikes or panicles, are so buried in protective wool that only the stamens are visible. There are about ten *Lachnostachys* species, all confined to southern Western Australia, where they are usually found on the sand plains. *Physopsis* is a genus of two species, also confined to the southwest. There are about a dozen *Newcastlia* species, mostly from the desert country of the west, with some extending into central Australia.

Pityrodia is another endemic genus; all except one, which occurs in the Kimberleys, are confined to the south of Western Australia. There are twenty-four species, commonly called native foxgloves, because of the tubular, curved, foxglove-type flowers, in various shades of pink, white, blue and purple. Foliage, as in other western members of the Verbena family, is densely felted. They occur in the drier parts of the State.

Another wholly western genus is *Cyanostegia*, with four species. These are the tinsel flowers, shrubs with blue, violet or purple flowers with papery, disc-like calyces. As these retain their form and bright colours long after the petals wither, the flowers have an 'everlasting' quality.

Plate 71
A NATIVE FOXGLOVE—*Pityrodia cuneata*
The native foxgloves, with their soft, felted leaves and tubular flowers, are plants of Western Australia's drier country. Flowers are various shades of pink, blue, purple and white; lobes are turned back in a two-lipped, foxglove-like fashion, and the throat is often spotted. *P. cuneata,* the one pictured, grows as a shrub, two to three metres high, in red sand on the heathlands north of Perth. It flowers in late winter and early spring.

Plate 72
A LAMBSTAIL—*Lachnostachys albicans*
The lambstail group of plants includes a number of genera within the Verbenaceae, mostly peculiar to Western Australia, with remarkable adaptations to a dry environment. Flowers are buried in dense woolly spikes, from which usually only the stamens protrude. Leaves are felted and sometimes crowded. The species pictured is an erect shrub, to one metre in height, fairly widespread on the sand plains of the southwest.

72

71

Family GOODENIACEAE

The Fan-flowers

Though Australia's flora is predominantly endemic so far as individual species and even genera are concerned, in the main the major plant families of other continents are also the major plant families here. An exception is the Goodeniaceae, an almost entirely Australian family of thirteen genera and over 300 species of herbs and under-shrubs. Members are widespread throughout the continent, but the major development is in the west: all of the genera and over two-thirds of the species occur there. Only a handful of species extend beyond Australia, some occurring in various Pacific islands and others ranging northward as far as South China.

Flowers of the Goodeniaceae usually have five sepals and a five-lobed, tubular corolla, usually split on one side, often giving the flowers the appearance of an open fan, or a hand with five spreading fingers. There are five stamens, free or with anthers united in a ring around the style, and a distinctive feature of the family is the indusium, a cup-shaped organ which surrounds and encloses the stigma. This ensures cross-pollination; stamens usually ripen while the flower is in bud, and as the style grows upwards, pollen is brushed from the anthers and collected in the cup-like surface of the indusium, while the immature stigma is still protected within it.

Best known of the Goodeniaceae is probably *Lechenaultia,* a genus of about twenty species, all confined to Western Australia except three, which extend across the continent. Largest genus is *Goodenia,* with about 120 species, found in all States and the Northern Territory. Western Australia has about sixty species, almost all of them being endemic. *Scaevola,* with sixty-nine endemic species, is also found in all States, but chiefly in Western Australia; this genus includes the strand plants of the sea coasts, and extends beyond Australia. The genus *Dampiera* commemorates William Dampier, who collected the first specimens when he visited the northwest coast of Australia in 1698. He commented on the prevalence of blue in the flora of New Holland, a factor well-illustrated by the genus named for him; flowers range in colour from palest blue to deepest purple. This is a purely Australian genus, most of the fifty-odd species being confined to the west.

Plate 75
BLUE LECHENAULTIA—*Lechenaultia biloba*
It is said the Aboriginals called this lechenaultia 'the floor of the sky', surely a most appropriate name for these flowers, which range in colour through almost every shade of clear blue seen in Australian skies, from limpid early morning to the brilliance of midday. Flowers are borne profusely from early winter to late summer; the deepest blue are usually found in gravel, and the paler forms in sand, in the drier areas. A low shrub, rarely more than fifty centimetres high, it has a wide range in southern and central Western Australia, and is one of six blue-flowered lechenaultias; other species are coloured flame red, orange and yellow, sometimes two-toned.

Plate 76
COMMON DAMPIERA—*Dampiera linearis*
The common dampiera is widespread from Geraldton to the south coast. It is a low, bushy perennial herb, fifteen to twenty-five centimetres in height, and flowers from mid-winter to mid-summer, most prolifically in spring. A distinguishing feature of *Dampiera* species is that the lower edges of the upper petals fold inwards, forming little ear-shaped receptacles (auricles) which collect and hold the ripe pollen.

75

76

Family STYLIDIACEAE

The Trigger-plants

Trigger-plants are herbs and small wiry shrubs, with a unique mechanism for ensuring effective cross-fertilisation of flowers. The family is predominantly Western Australian, for over eighty per cent of the total number of species are found there, most of them belonging to the one genus, *Stylidium*. Flowers are bisexual, with five sepals and five petals, the corolla tubular, consisting of two pairs of spreading lobes and a fifth, much smaller and inconspicuous, which forms a small lip. Flowers are usually white, pink or yellow, and the inflorescence is terminal. Leaves are usually tufted and grass-like. There are about 140 species of *Stylidium*, over 100 of which are recorded from Western Australia. The popular name, 'trigger-plants' refers to the sensitive curved column in which the style and two stamens are fused. Anthers and stigma mature at different times, so that the column at first conveys pollen, then receives it.

During this period it is normally bent sharply back below the petals, 'set' like the spring of a mousetrap. When an insect alights at the base, the column whips smartly back across the flower, showering the visitor with pollen to be carried on its way, or collecting that gathered at the previous port-of-call, depending on the stage of maturity.

The column then moves back and re-sets itself, continuing to do so until the whole process of pollen transfer is completed and the flower itself is fertilised, when the column loses its elasticity. The only other western genus of this family is *Levenhookia*, with eight species, seven of which are indigenous to Western Australia. These are dwarf annuals, found mainly in swamps.

Plate 77
A TRIGGER-PLANT—*Stylidium schoenoides*
The trigger plants are dainty, attractive flowers in their own right, but the main interest in the group is the sensitive column, consisting of fused style and stamens, which is bent sharply when set; the base is sensitive when the pollen is ripe, and springs sideways when touched by an alighting insect, showering it with pollen from the anthers or picking up pollen from another flower on the sticky stigma. *S. scoenoides* is a tufted plant, fifteen to thirty centimetres high, found in sandy situations in the south generally.

Plate 78
CIRCUS TRIGGER-PLANT—*Stylidium bulbiferum*
The circus trigger-plant is a small creeping mat-like plant which bears masses of pink, red or white flowers, mainly in spring. It grows on sand and gravel from Geraldton to the south coast.

77

78

Family ASTERACEAE
(formerly Compositae)

The Daisies

The daisy family is the largest family of flowering plants in the world, and also the most widespread. There are probably 1,000 genera and over 20,000 species. They are found in all parts of the globe, in habitats ranging from alpine to desert. Members are mainly herbs, though climbers, shrubs and even trees occur. Included within this family are ornamentals such as asters, chrysanthemums, dahlias, zinnias, marigolds and cornflowers, as well as the traditional daisy. Weeds such as dandelions, cobblers' pegs and Bathurst burrs are members, and plants of economic importance—the chicory of commerce, vegetables such as lettuce and artichoke, sunflowers, the seeds of which yield edible oil, and pyrethrum, source of an insect repellant. Numerically, the family is the third largest in Australia, exceeded only by the Myrtaceae and the Proteaceae. There are probably at least 800 indigenous species, representing about 100 genera, and about half of these are found in the west.

Flowers of the Asteraceae are clustered into heads, attached to a common base and surrounded by one or several rows of bracts which perform the function of sepals, protecting the composite inflorescence in bud. In the individual flowers, sepals are replaced by hairs, bristles or scales (known botanically as pappus) or are absent. There are five petals, united into a corolla but showing their origin in five lobes or teeth. Sometimes the corolla is tubular, with five regular lobes, and sometimes it is ligulate, that is, with the upper part extended in a tongue-like, toothed strap. Some-

times the flowerhead consists entirely of tubular florets, as in the little 'billy buttons' (*Craspedia* species). Sometimes they are all ligulate, as in dandelions. More often, as in the familiar daisy, there is a central disc of tubular flowers (called disc florets) surrounded by a ray of petal-like ligulate flowers (called ray florets). In these mixed types the disc florets are usually bisexual, while the ray florets are female or neuter—their main function, like that of petals in flowers of other families, being to attract pollinating insects.

Amongst devices which have assisted the daisies to become the largest family in the plant world is the rosette of flat, radical leaves formed at the base of many species—commandeering surrounding soil and depriving competitors of sunlight. Methods of distribution of seeds are also most efficient. Frequently, as in dandelions, the pappus (modified sepals) is hairy or silky, so that the whole structure

Plate 79
ROSY SUNRAY—*Helipterum roseum*
A slender, upright annual, this everlasting of dry inland areas is commonly cultivated, and massed displays may be seen in Kings Gardens, Perth, where those pictured were photographed. The central disc of florets may be yellow to black, and the involucre of soft, papery bracts which surround it varies in colour from white to rosy pink or red. The two distinct types can be seen in this photograph. *Helipterum* is a genus of about sixty Australian species, found chiefly in inland areas of all States and the Northern Territory. It differs from *Helichrysum,* which it closely resembles, in the structure of the pappus and the fact that the involucral bracts are softer to the touch and appear more numerous.

acts like a parachute, enabling the seeds to be carried by the wind. In other cases, the pappus consists of stiff, barbed bristles, which cling to passing animals (the common weed, cobbler's peg, is an example).

Western Australian genera include desert 'everlastings' such as *Helichrysum'* (paper daisies) and *Helipterum* (sunrays)—flowers with papery involucral bracts often radiating beyond the composite head in a petal-like fashion; traditional daisy-like plants such as *Brachycome, Senecio, Olearia;* and genera such as *Myriocephalus* and *Craspedia,* where the inflorescence consists of a number of small heads of tubular flowers, grouped together into a button-like dome or large flat disc. *Helichrysum* is a genus of about 300 species, well distributed throughout the world. Australia has about 100, all endemic, twenty-six of which occur in the west. *Craspedia* is a genus of four species, all confined to Australia; two are found in the west. *Senecio* is the largest genus in the family, with more than 1,300 species, ranging over nearly all the world. Australia has about forty, all yellow-flowered, nine of which occur in Western Australia. *Brachycome* is a mainly Australian genus of about sixty species (fourteen in Western Australia). They are to be found in all States and the Northern Territory, growing under conditions varying from near-desert to alpine. Leaves often form rosettes and the solitary flowerheads are borne on long stems. Flowers are very like those of the English daisy, and indeed the two genera are closely allied. *Olearia* is a mainly Australian genus of shrubs and undershrubs (rarely small trees), closely allied to the old world *Aster.* There are about eighty indigenous species, widely distributed throughout the continent, with about twenty-five in the west. Most of the remaining species are confined to New Zealand and a few occur in the highlands of New Guinea.

Plate 80
PRO-CUMENT ANGIANTHUS—
Angianthus humifusus
A prostrate herb of the sand heaths of the southwest, this member of the daisy family has numerous white flowerheads crowded in a dense compound terminal head. *Angianthus* is an Australian genus of about thirty species, the majority of which occur in Western Australia.

Plate 81
A SUNRAY—*Helipterum condensatum*
This *Helipterum* is a dense tufted herb, found on the northwest coast between Shark Bay and Exmouth Gulf. The one pictured was photographed on Peron Peninsula in September.

Plate 82
SPLENDID EVERLASTING—*Helipterum splendidum*
The largest of the paper daisies, this *Helipterum* has white to creamy-yellow flowers, carried in solitary heads five centimetres or more across. It grows in the mulga and spinifex country, from the northwest coast to the fringe of the inland deserts, blooming profusely after the winter rains.

Plate 83
FRAGRANT EVERLASTING—*Waitzia suaveolens*
The everlasting daisies of the genus *Waitzia* have flowerheads surrounded by stiff papery floral bracts, white, yellow or pink, which retain their form and colour when dried. There are six species, all Western Australian and all endemic except one which extends to South Australia and the eastern States. The species pictured is a slender herb or undershrub, to thirty centimetres high, and is confined to the southwest.

80

81

82

83

GLOSSARY

anther: the part of the stamen which contains pollen.

auricle: ear-shaped lobe at base of leaf, petal or other organ.

axil: angle formed by leaf and branch.

axis: stem or central part.

berry: fleshy fruit with seeds immersed in pulp.

bipinnate: leaves twice divided in a pinnate manner.

bract: modified leaf associated with a flower or inflorescence.

calyx (pl, *calyces*): the sepals collectively; the outer whorl of floral leaves.

capsule: dry fruit of two or more united carpels, which opens when ripe.

carpel: the female organ of the flower, composed of ovary, style and stigma.

corolla: the petals collectively; the inner whorl of floral leaves.

cyme: an inflorescence with the oldest flowers towards the centre, often with each branch ending in a flower and younger flowers arising at lower branches.

drupe: a succulent fruit with a hard stone.

endemic: confined to a particular geographical region and found nowhere else.

filament: stalk of the stamen.

follicle: dry, one-seeded fruit formed from a single pistil which splits open when ripe.

fruit: seed-bearing structure consisting of mature ovary and any additional parts of the flower which may remain attached to it.

genus (pl, *genera*): a group in biological classification, consisting of one or more species.

glabrous: without hairs.

herb: a plant which does not produce a woody stem.

inflorescence: the disposition of the flowers on the floral axis.

involucre, involucral bracts: a whorl of bracts below or around the inflorescence.

lignotuber: a woody swelling at the base of a stem, which stores food and has dormant buds.

ligulate: strap-shaped.

linear: long, narrow, with parallel sides.

monotypic: having only one member.

nut: dry, one-seeded fruit which does not split open when mature.

operculum: cap of fused petals or perianth segments covering a flower bud; the lid of a capsule which opens by a circular split.

ovary: the basal part of the pistil or female organ, in which the seeds develop.

palmate leaf: divided into leaflets, the leaflets diverging from a central point.

panicle: much-branched inflorescence, a series of racemes.

perianth: calyx (sepals) and corolla (petals) collectively.

phyllodes: flattened leaf stalks which are leaf-like and perform the function of leaves.

pinnate: compound leaf with leaflets arranged on each side of a common stalk; feather-like.

pistil: the female part of a flower, usually consisting of ovary, style, and stigma; one or more carpels (where there is only one carpel, the terms are synonymous).

raceme: inflorescence of stalked flowers, with the youngest flowers nearest the apex.

schizocarp: dry fruit which when ripe divides into several one-seeded carpels.

sclerophyll: plants with hard, stiff foliage.

sepals: the outer whorl of the flower, usually green; known collectively as calyx.

species: a group in biological classification, consisting of plants possessing distinctive characteristics.

spike: inflorescence of stalkless flowers, the youngest flowers nearest the apex.

stamen: male part of the flower, consisting of filament and anther.

stigma: that part of the female organ of the flower adapted for the reception of pollen.

stipules: pair of small appendages at the base of a leaf-insertion in certain plants.

style: that part of the female organ of the flower situated above the ovary and bearing the stigma.

tepals: individual perianth segments, particularly where corolla and calyx are not clearly differentiated.

trifoliate: having three leaflets.

umbel: an inflorescence with all flower stalks arising from a common point, often flat-topped.

unisexual: either male or female; a flower with stamens or pistil but not both.

valvate: with edges touching but not overlapping.

INDEX

Light figures indicate text page reference, bold figures indicate colour plate page references.